LETTING GO OF

THE PERSON YOU

USED TO BE

ALSO BY LAMA SURYA DAS

Awakening the Buddhist Heart
Awakening to the Sacred
Awakening the Buddha Within
The Snow Lion's Turquoise Mane
Natural Great Perfection
(with Nyoshul Khenpo Rinpoche)

Lessons on Change,
Loss, and Spiritual
Transformation

Broadway Books New York

LETTING GO OF
THE PERSON YOU
USED TO BE

Lama Surya Das

BROADWAY

A hardcover edition of this book was published
in 2003 by Broadway Books.

LETTING GO OF THE PERSON YOU USED TO BE.
Copyright © 2003 by Lama Surya Das. All rights reserved.
No part of this book may be reproduced or transmitted in any form
or by any means, electronic or mechanical, including photocopying,
recording, or by any information storage and retrieval system, without
written permission from the publisher. For information, address
Broadway Books, a division of Random House, Inc.

PRINTED IN THE UNITED STATES OF AMERICA

BROADWAY BOOKS and its logo, a letter B bisected on the diagonal,
are trademarks of Random House, Inc.

Visit our website at www.broadwaybooks.com

First trade paperback edition published November 2004

Book design by Dana Leigh Treglia

The Library of Congress has cataloged
the hardcover edition as follows:

Das, Surya.
Letting go of the person you used to be : lessons on change,
loss, and spiritual transformation / Lama Surya Das.—1st ed.
p.   cm.
Includes index.
I. Title
BQ567.D37   2003
294.3'4442—dc21   2002043682

ISBN 0-7679-0874-0

1   3   5   7   9   10   8   6   4   2

To the long life of the Dalai Lama and

the freedom and well-being of

the people of Tibet

Contents

Introduction:
Gaining Through Loss

Wherever I go lately, people ask how I deal with fear, anger, and pain; they want advice on healing painful wounds caused by trauma and shock in their lives. It seems as though I am speaking and writing constantly about the need for learning to grieve, to learn the lessons, to let go and forgive and move on; and for prayerful reflection, more historical learning, and cross-cultural global perspectives. Many of us are seeking a common ground and higher spiritual principles to adhere to during troubled times. I firmly believed that deep down everyone truly wants peaceful coexistence in this world in our lifetime. But we must first learn how to deal with anger and hatred in ourselves, to soften and disarm our own hearts, before we can effectively work to resolve conflicts and create peace with others.

Many men and women are reeling emotionally from recent traumas, whether these traumas represent personal disappointment and loss or global chaos. Too frequently, the common "advice" we hear for dealing with our feelings of grief and pain falls short of really helping. Retaliation, revenge, and anger, while they might seem initially satisfying, are not the answers. Neither are despair and helplessness. But there is a middle-way approach, in which suffering can be transformed into understanding, compassion, wisdom, and even peace. This is possible for all of us if we apply ourselves to such a transformation, no matter who we are, where we live, or what we believe. Reverend Martin Luther King said that we have only two choices: "to live together as brothers or perish together as fools." It is inevitably in our higher self-interest to pull together, if we don't want to be pulled apart.

Buddha taught that without any difficulties and problems, we cannot really grow in inner strength, patient forbearance, emotional maturity, and vision. Everything changes, yet what is most true and real always remains. This has been brought home to me in recent years. I have learned that "If you truly want to grow as a person and learn, you should realize that the universe has enrolled you in the graduate program of life, called loss," as Dr. Elisabeth Kubler-Ross says.

There is a story about a seeker who travels to the Himalayas, looking for an enlightened Buddha in order to receive personal teachings. This seeker wants the last word on the subject of enlightenment. Walking and trekking for days, he begins to drop his heavy gear as he makes his way to the top of a high peak in Nepal. He drops his tent, his camping equipment, and his heavy backpack. Stripped of almost everything and having breathed so many hundreds of thousands of breaths, he has finally forgotten about his worldly preoccupations. He is very ready to arrive and very ready to listen. He pulls himself up over the final rim of the mountain and looks into the mouth of a cave. Amazingly enough, the Buddha-like master is sitting right there. Stunned, relieved, and overjoyed, the seeker asks the Sage, "What is the first principle? What is your most important truth and teaching?"

The seeker thinks this is going to be his big moment and that he is about to become enlightened. He is going to discover the one essential thing for him to ponder. And then the Buddha replies: "Dukkha. Life is suffering, life is fraught, life is difficult." And the seeker is totally disappointed! He looks around wildly and shouts, "Is there anyone else up here that I can talk to?!!"

I love that story. What do we do when we experience something that isn't quite what we had hoped for, or worse, when we experience something that is truly difficult? Fortunately, within the Buddhist canon there are many wonderful teachings that provide guidance for us. The teachings help us deal intelligently with loss, change, and fear; they help us with the big questions, like the meaning of life and the keys to happiness; and they teach us about death and suffering, and how to utilize everything as grist for the mill and as the means for transformation.

A Buddhist wise guy's rendition of the First Noble Truth of dukkha (dissatisfaction) is that in life pain is inevitable, but suffering is optional. How much we suffer depends on us, our internal development, and our spiritual understanding and realization. Our pain and suffering point out to us where we are most attached to ourselves—our body, for example, or our loved ones; it shows us what we are holding on to the most. By recognizing this, we can learn to use loss and suffering in ways that help us to grow wiser and become more at peace with ourselves and the universe.

I believe that this is the time to become warriors for peace and dialogue, not warmongers or mere worriers. We must learn the hard lesson that without the pain of inner irritation, the pearls of wisdom will not be produced within us. I lovingly call this The Pearl Principle: no pain, no transformative gain.

Inside an oyster, it takes an irritant—like a grain of sand or a bit of shell—to stimulate the oyster to produce the mucous juices that engulf and surround the irritant, eventually hardening into a precious pearl. It is the same for us, regardless of how much we wish it to be otherwise. Difficulties and suffering produce the aspiration for spiritual enlightenment, and it is this aspiration which is needed to motivate us along the path of awakening and liberation. There is no growth without growing pains—and the labor pains of giving birth to a new world and a new way of being can be the most painful yet rewarding of all.

I find that the Buddhist virtue, or paramita (transcendental perfection), that is most essential, most helpful for dealing with pain, difficulty, and suffering, is patience. The fourth paramita, *Shanti*, advocates patience, forbearance, acceptance, tolerance, forgiveness, and allowing. It requires a certain kind of expansion, a generous embracing and merging, rather than retracting and separating. It takes a lot of time, patience, and fortitude, but I think Shanti helps me the most to bear pain and sorrow. It takes courage and stamina to hang in there, but it's worth it in the long run.

Face your difficulties realistically, rather than withdrawing from them, and riches can be yours. When faced with pain and misfortune, simply stop and center yourself in the present moment, here and now; take a deep breath, sit down and concentrate; pray. Or try to laugh, one way or another. Laugh the cosmic laugh, lighten up, and be en-lightened.

Lama Surya Das
Cambridge, Massachusetts
January 2003

LETTING GO OF
THE PERSON YOU
USED TO BE

CHAPTER ONE

Making Sense of
the Madness

Why does God allow guns? Why did Jonathan's daddy have to die?
Why was Margaret born blind?

AMELIA,

four years old

Why is there illness, death, and suffering? Why are we separated from those we love? Why is there pain? Why do bad things happen? Why do people hurt each other? Why is life so filled with loss? And the universal question: Why do bad things happen to me? Stuff happens—everyone knows that—but why does it happen to me, why am I so often in the midst of it!

No one has fully satisfactory or verifiable answers to any of these questions. We don't really know. This is part of the great mystery of life. Sure, there are many possible theories and explanations. I have friends, for example, who are astrology buffs. They say that the world events that began on September 11, 2001, were put in motion by an opposition between the planets Pluto and Saturn. It was written in the stars.

Some people are adamant about personifying evil. When we look around us we see leaders from all persuasions referring to those who disagree with them as being evil and followers of the devil. There are men and women who blame everything on Satan himself, who they envision as a real, albeit unseen, entity, who malevolently waltzes through our world, taking advantage of our weaknesses, which of course causes all varieties of havoc. I picked up the newspaper one day last year and read a statement from a fundamentalist preacher who said that some of our most serious problems are well deserved and come about because we are sinners with questionable sexual proclivities. This kind of simplistic fundamentalism has never had much appeal for me. It doesn't even make sense. In fact I think it is a crock, and I don't mind saying so.

Schopenhauer, one of my favorite philosophers, said: "Life is endless pain with a painful end." But is that all, I wonder? It's a sad and frustrating fact that much of the time we can't make sense of the unhappiness of our lives. Some events are easy to comprehend and can be directly attributable to cause and effect. We drive carelessly, for example, and we have accidents. This makes sense. But random events do occur, and cautious people are also in serious accidents. Cautious people are driving in the wrong place at the wrong time; cautious people are also hurt. Things happen that don't seem fair. Why? Are there underlying explanations for this? If I were to answer this question, I would have to say— probably. Everything has a cause or causes, but I certainly don't always know what they are. Nor do I think that anyone else does. The reasons why we are hurt by life are often as mysterious as the reasons why we are graced with beauty and joy. This all belongs in the category of the unknowable. Much in the universe is inscrutable and unfathomable. Omniscience would help us grasp these matters, but it is in short supply in the human realm.

I am a Buddhist and, as such, I accept the reality of karma and the law of cause and effect. It makes good sense to me. But I also know that the laws of karma are far more complex than any simple sitcom version. We are living not only with our own personal karma, but also with the karma of every other being we meet. When my karma meets your karma, something happens. And, of course, it isn't only about individual karma; there is group karma as well. In this speeded-up world, where we have access to the CNN crawl and minute-by-minute news broadcasts from around the world, think about the karmic repercussions. Shooting breaks out between Israelis and Palestinians on the West Bank. A traumatized tourist with a video camera gives the footage to CNN. It is on the air within the hour. Someplace in Montana, a young mother, making a peanut butter and jelly sandwich for her five year old, is watching. She gets so upset that she drops the jar of jelly, which crashes to the floor. Her barefoot little girl walks in the kitchen at that moment and cuts her toe. More blood flows. How is this all karmically connected? It's impenetrable to mere mortals. "The beauty of the world has two edges, one of laughter, one of anguish, cutting the heart asunder." Virginia Woolf said that.

Only omniscient awareness can totally comprehend causation with all its details, interconnections, and ramifications. The Buddha said that only an omniscient Buddha, a perfectly enlightened and fully awakened being, could understand the myriad causes and conditions that bring about the color of a single peacock's feather.

Since we are not omniscient, since we have limited view and weak foresight, we don't know exactly why things happen. However we do know that it is impossible to avoid all of life's negative experiences. Recently I was standing in a corner coffee shop, waiting at the cash register to pay my bill when a distraught couple came into the restaurant. Both the man and the woman were very excited and talking rapidly. They reminded the cashier that when they left the restaurant about an hour earlier, they had been accompanied by their eighteen-month-old toddler. At the time the little boy had been clutching his favorite stuffed animal—a small purple cow. Whey they arrived home and tucked the sleeping child into his crib, they discovered that he had loosened his grip on his furry toy. Now the purple cow was missing! What could have happened to it?

The couple had hastily arranged for a neighbor to stay with the child, and they were now frantically retracing their footsteps in an attempt to recover the cherished toy. They were hoping against hope that someone had turned it in to the restaurant cashier.

"He's going to be so upset when he wakes up and finds that it's gone!" the father said.

"He loves that cow! He never goes anywhere without it. I knew I should have tried to find another one to buy just in case this happened," the mother said.

"I should have been paying more attention," the father blames himself. "How could I have let this happen?"

The cashier queried various employees. Everyone was very sympathetic. Who hasn't lost something precious and beloved? Who doesn't identify with the pain of childhood losses? Who couldn't empathize with these doting parents who wanted to spare their toddler the pain associated with loss?

More than 2,500 years ago in ancient India, on the border of what is now Nepal, there was another parent who wanted his child to live a pain-free life. His name was King Suddhodana, and he was the father of the man, born as Siddhartha, who we now know as Gautama, the Buddha. Suddhodana was a powerful leader, wealthy enough to build a walled castle filled with flower gardens, elegant food, gracious furnishings, beautiful music, and great luxury.

Legend has it that before Siddhartha, the child who was to become the Buddha, was born, his mother had a dream: She saw her son as a great spiritual warrior, a radiant Bodhisattva who was transformed into a white elephant. The elephant climbed a golden mountain, then a silver mountain, and finally, carrying a white lotus in his trunk, touched the mother on her side. The white elephant then dissolved like vapor into her pregnant womb.

The seers summoned to interpret the dream told the king that the child who was to be born would either be a universal ruler or an enlightened sage, a Buddha. Like many parents, the king wanted his son to follow in his footsteps; he didn't relish the notion of raising a child who would renounce the world in favor of monasticism and a homeless mendicant's begging bowl. With that in mind, the wise men issued a warning: If the king wanted his son to embrace a royal vocation, he must make certain that the young prince never left home, for if he went forth into the world, he would see suffering. Then he would most certainly be moved to become a spiritual seeker.

Because Suddhodana wanted his son to live the life of a

prince, not an ascetic, he decided that he would protect his son from the sight of any suffering. Then, as now, the world was filled with poverty, pain, injustice, sickness, and death. To make sure that his beloved child never came in contact with the miserable aspects of life, the king determined to keep his son in the palace surrounded by high walls and provided with all the luxuries of life. And whenever the young prince appeared reflective or questioned the meaning of life, the king ordered more lavish sporting competitions and entertainments, reminding everyone that the prince was never to go out beyond the palace walls. Suddhodana was a loving parent; he wanted desperately to shield his son from unhappiness. And, of course, he couldn't, because eventually the young prince Siddhartha convinced his faithful charioteer to take him out into the city. That's when Siddhartha saw those things that he had been sheltered from his entire life. Siddhartha saw a sick man, an elderly crippled man, and a corpse at the cremation ground; for the first time, he saw poverty and pain.

When he ventured beyond his father's palace walls, Siddhartha suddenly became aware of the range of human suffering. Think about how deeply the young prince's innate compassionate heart must have been touched by what he saw. Siddhartha lost his precious innocence. He lost the ability to avoid or deny reality and the fact of the misery that was on display among the people around him. With these losses, everything in Siddhartha's world changed; he became thoughtful and restless. He was disturbed by what he had viewed. Siddhartha's encounter with loss readied and prepared him for what he saw on his next trip outside the palace walls. That's when Siddhartha met a wandering ascetic Hindu holy man, a peaceful and radiant sadhu, who seemed to have made peace with life. Siddhartha realized that he needed to understand more about the cyclic nature of life and death; he wanted to find answers that would remedy universal pain and suffering. He made the decision to seek truth on the spiritual path and give up the life he had in favor of the new life that awaited him. He slipped out of his father's palace in the middle of night, under the cover of darkness, while the devas and angels, using their soft wings, muffled the sound of his horse's footsteps.

These four sights, representing sickness, aging, death, and peace, are said by history to be the turning point of youthful Prince Siddhartha's iconic life. Siddhartha's response to the loss of innocence points out something that most of us know. Whenever we lose something—anything—we come to one of life's little crossroads. With every loss or separation comes the possibility of change, growth, and transformation. Each loss provides a genuine opportunity for learning. We can gain through loss if we open ourselves to this counterintuitive jewel. This is the positive kernel that is potentially contained in each loss that any one of us suffers, like the inner irritant that can produce a lustrous pearl.

I love the story of how the young man who was to become the enlightened Buddha stepped onto the spiritual path. He did so because he wanted to help alleviate suffering. He wanted to find a way to transform pain into peace and wisdom. He didn't think just about himself, but felt instinctively compelled to seek universal deliverance.

Have you ever experienced a serious loss and thought to yourself, There must be a reason why I'm going through this. What is it that I need to learn? Most of us have. Historian Daniel Boorstin calls man "the asking animal." Spiritual seekers particularly are on a quest to understand life; we want to examine our own lives and find meaning in what we do and who we are. We ask, "Who am I and why do I exist?" Like the Buddha, we want to find the lessons that lie buried in suffering and pain. Questioning is an essential part of the spiritual path: self-inquiry, introspection, philosophy—all involve genuine doubt and skepticism as propellants fueling the spiritual journey. We find meaning in the seeking itself. Every step along the way is the Way, full of purpose, however veiled or dimly perceived. Science tells us about the heavens and where they are; religion tells us how to get to heaven. Yet Einstein said that he thought the most beautiful thing in the world was the mysterious—the great question mark. The great "why?" Why do we seek, why do we ask, doubt, wonder? *Because.* Because we must.

Seekers inevitably want to get a better handle on life; we want to figure things out. We know intuitively that the events of our lives are not always arbitrary. We feel connected, however intangibly. We know that it is in our higher self-interest to unravel the mysteries in our own lives. There must be a higher purpose and greater meaning. As we become more and more spiritually evolved, we become more determined to find wisdom and reach a deeper understanding of our lives and our paths.

Not that long ago, I saw a rerun of a television interview with Mattie Stepanek, the incredibly wise child poet who published a book called *Journey Through Heartsongs.* Mattie, who is confined to a wheelchair, has been stricken with a disease that has already killed his siblings. He needs help in performing many bodily functions, including breathing itself. The interviewer asked Mattie if he ever felt sorry for himself, and he answered that he had of course experienced "Why me?" reactions. But then this brilliant child followed up this thought with a larger and more profound question. He then said, "Why not me?" He went on to tell the interviewer that he felt that he might be better equipped to handle his illness than some others. This child is clearly a spiritual prodigy. Tibetans would quickly point out that this kind of spiritual genius comes from a past life. We could all do well to learn what Mattie instinctively understands. As the Sufis say, "When the heart grieves for what is lost, the spirit rejoices over what it has left."

WORKING ON OURSELVES

Men and women who are in therapy are familiar with the phrase, "working on yourself." When we do "work" on ourselves we are trying to become stronger, more accepting of ourselves, and more internally resilient. We are trying to further develop our mental health and well being. The spiritual path is similarly filled with inner and outer work. The promise of transformation and even ultimate enlightenment exists, but only if we do the necessary work. Mysteries unfold and reveal themselves slowly but surely. When we are adolescents, for example, we don't really know what love is. Our judgment, hormones, and swirling feelings are all confused and often in conflict. We're interested in figuring things out, although much of the time we're pretty much in the dark. As we get older we begin to be better able to see through the murk. If we are paying attention and practicing some form of self-reflection, experience will gradually give us greater clarity and wisdom.

In some ways, every single one of us has a life that resembles the infamous Augean stable. The Augean stable, you will remember, was the indescribably filthy stable that Hercules was assigned to clean as one of his twelve legendary tasks. Like Hercules, we all have a lot of junk to wade through and sort out. We have so much to do, and there are days when we feel as though there is so much chaos and confusion that we don't even know where to begin. That is a good starting point.

Working on ourselves when we are in the middle of our own chaos and distress is a challenging task. But what else is there to do? To simply gloss over our problems and go into denial isn't going to help. There must be something we can learn from our current difficulties. Even if we don't understand all of it, we know that each of us has his or her own path and karma to work out. It's up to us to make the most of the opportunities that are given to us. Enlightened spiritual masters always remind their students that suffering and loss can help us grow spiritually. We can grow in wisdom and use our personal challenges as tools to transform our lives. Keep the image of Hercules in mind; by meeting his challenges, he became divine.

My Tibetan teachers always told me that the first step in

handling suffering was to look at our losses realistically. Put aside all illusions and delusions about what could have been or should have been. Then squarely face the grief and the pain. Acknowledge your tears and unhappiness. Know what you are experiencing. This is the opposite of denial. Feel it, examine it, and reflect upon it. Sense directly in the present moment how it affects you in your body and your mind. Reflect on the ways that you can use your loss to grow spiritually. Is it all entirely negative or it is just unwanted? Are you suffering greatly from disappointment and resistance to change? How can you grow and develop from your travail? How can you relinquish what is negative and adopt what is wholesome and positive? Sooner or later this internal investigation will bring about different, more salutary results.

When we lose things we care about, we can gain a deeper understanding about what is important. One of my old friends from India ashram days is the spiritual teacher and old soul, Ram Dass, whose writings and lectures helped introduce so many Westerners to the Wisdom of the East. Ram Dass always prided himself on being independent and self-sufficient. He was always powerful, smart, successful, and resourceful. He was a Harvard professor, researcher, writer, and pioneering spirit—a veritable scout on the frontiers of human consciousness, bringing back the news of the infinite possibilities available to all of us. Ram Dass tried always to be a selfless servant of God, humanity, and the world. Then a couple of years ago, while in his sixties, Ram Dass suffered a serious stroke and almost died. Afterward he was impaired. Everything changed for him.

Ram Dass acknowledges that he had always been drawn to power, and now he is suffering from his new limitations. He had always felt gratified at helping others; now he finds it hard to accept help and to be so helpless. He says that he had sought to escape his humanity by realizing divinity, partly so as not to feel vulnerable. And suddenly he feels so very vulnerable and dependent on those around him.

The last time I talked to Ram Dass, he told me that his newly discovered vulnerability—frightening as it was, or as it had once seemed—was furthering his own humanity; it was helping him grow in love and connection with others. He said that he had come to the startling conclusion that when he had a stroke his guru and God "had stroked him." "It must be a teaching," he says. And, as a true devotee, he wanted to see what he could, should, and must learn from this intense new experience and challenging period of his life.

Ram Dass is still exploring the leading edge, bringing back to us the news from the front. In his most recent book, *Still Here,* in a chapter aptly titled "Stroke Yoga," Ram Dass writes: "Krishna taught Arjuna in the *Bhagavad Gita* how to use the battles of life to come to God. My stroke is one of those battles. It's hard stuff. The stroke raised the bar because it entailed so much suffering, but greater suffering elicits higher consciousness. It was (my guru) Maharaji who turned up the pressure for me to 'get it,' and it moved the game to a different league. . . . I'd like to bring myself and everyone else to that Awareness—that's always been my central purpose. The stroke took away a lot of ego distractions, and brought me back to my Soul's purpose. That's what healing is all about."

In a letter written back in 1819, the British poet John Keats refers to the world not as a vale of tears, but as "the vale of soul-making." He says, "Do you not see how necessary a World of Pains and Troubles is to school an intelligence and make it a Soul? A Place where the heart must feel and suffer in a thousand diverse ways!"

I realize that when we are grieving and struggling, the knowledge that we are gaining in inner strength and fortitude offers little in the way of consolation. Melanie, who last year lost her husband, the father of her two small children, says: "When my husband died, my heart broke. I can still feel the pain in my chest. Sure I've learned to be strong, but who needs to be this strong? To tell you the truth, I never wanted to be this strong."

Sometimes men and women who experience great loss end

up being shocked and surprised by their own strength and resilience even when facing losses that seem impossible to bear. The Buddha was once approached by a grieving mother whose little child had just died. She pleaded with him for a miracle: She begged him to restore the child to her alive and well. The Buddha listened to the bereaved woman and finally said that he would be able to do what she asked if she could bring him a mustard seed from a home that had never lost anyone to death. The mother traveled far and wide, day after day, trying to find such a home, and of course she couldn't. Finally she returned to the Buddha and said that she had come to realize that death visits everyone. It was a reality she had to accept. And in that acceptance she found strength and consolation. Eventually, through meditating on the cycle of birth, illness, aging, and death, she realized wisdom and liberation. This is the blessing of gaining spiritual experience and maturity.

Loss is the great equalizer that reminds us that we are not omnipotent; it helps us crack open our defensive shell of invulnerability and denial. It helps us see the ways that we avoid the truth of our human frailty and rely on a false sense of control. There is no question but that loss can have spiritual benefits. Loss makes us more sensitive and aware. We become aware of our own pain and, in so doing, we have an opportunity to extend our understanding of suffering and become more compassionate toward others. I'm always tremendously impressed and moved by organizations like MADD (Mothers Against Drunk Driving), for example. How inspiring it is to see people who can channel the pain in their own lives into something that can and will benefit others.

One doesn't necessarily need to start a national organization in order to make lemonade out of lemons in this way. My friend Bob, for example, was never particularly sensitive to people who were sick. Then he suffered a serious back injury that required surgery and a long rehabilitation. After he got out of the hospital, he had a completely new attitude about what people who are ill experience. He began to volunteer in hospitals, he went out of his way to donate blood regularly, and he signed up to be a bone marrow donor. Now whenever someone he knows is hospitalized or undergoing long-term treatment, Bob makes a point of visiting; he brings cookies or reading material; he calls and sends e-mail. He says he knows firsthand what it feels like to be scared and dependent on medical personnel, and he wants to help. His experience sensitized him in a real way.

We hate the idea of loss because we know what loss represents.

Loss = pain. Loss = suffering. Loss = unhappiness.

We cry because of our losses; we despair and become depressed because of our losses; we lose hope because of our losses. We are haunted by our losses and we often define ourselves by our losses. But, and this is an important but, we are also strengthened by our losses. We can change and mature spiritually because of our losses.

Almost by definition, loss is transformative. Many seekers have stepped onto the spiritual path because of a searing loss in their lives. For some it's the death of a loved one; for others it's the loss of a dream or career plan; for many it's a relationship breakup and the loss of romantic love. These people may feel as though their hearts are breaking; they can almost touch the break and envision the little zigzag line, much like cartoon valentine depictions.

Some men and women respond to suffering and personal pain by becoming hardened, constricted, and embittered; they become more self-centered and less aware of the pain experienced by the rest of the world. But those who are wiser and more spiritually evolved respond differently. They are able to view their losses more realistically. They get past numbness and despair; they get past bitterness; and they get past their initial "Why me?" reactions. Even though bad things continue to happen to them and those they love, they choose to walk the spiritual path and search for meaning and inner wisdom amid the madness. Their losses helped point them in the right direction, toward a deeper dimension of reality; their pain and suffering brought them in closer touch with their own inner goodness and its natural connection to the divine.

A story I first heard in India reflects some of the problems we face when trying to find meaning and wisdom.

It seems there was a young spiritual student who became impatient with the teachings he was receiving from the master in his own village. He wanted to know everything, and he wanted that information immediately. He went to his village master and demanded to be told the final truth about God.

The teacher responded by saying that the truth that he was seeking was simply that he, the student, was God. God, truth, and meaning were to be found within.

At this the young man became outraged and indignant. He felt that the master's answer was preposterous. But the master was unwavering in what he had to say, and so the student left the village in search of a different teaching. The student sought out gurus and masters far and wide, but no matter how renowned or wise these teachers were said to be, all of them in the end gave the student the same answer about life—that he was God. This wasn't what he wanted to hear; in fact, he saw this answer as an indication of the teachers' incompetence.

Finally he came upon a new teacher to whom he vehemently complained about his previous gurus and related his concerns. This wise teacher was very understanding and reassuring. He told the student that the truth about God would be revealed to him, but not immediately. He said that it would take some years, under the teacher's guidance, for the student's realization to come forth. Because the student was too poor to remain with the teacher for instruction, he arranged a work-study exchange. The only job available was shoveling manure all day in the field. The student gladly accepted this job and persisted steadily for seven years in this endeavor. Finally, at the end of the seventh year, the student came to the teacher and demanded some satisfaction.

"All right," the teacher said. "You have toiled long and hard, and you deserve to hear the truth. Know then that the truth you seek is just this: You are God."

The student became enraged and said, "How could this be? How could it be that you are just the same as all the other fools who told me this. And if this is the case, why have I toiled in your fields for these many years?"

"Because, my diligent student," the master said, "although you are indeed God, you are simply not very bright."

The long-suffering student of this tale provides an interesting lesson. The student, in this instance, has great purpose, and he is absolutely heroic in his pursuit of truth. He does backbreaking and heartbreaking work for years. We wonder what his teacher's purpose is in asking so much of the student: Does the master hope that these years of service work will open the student's eyes and remove his karmic obscurations? Will the simple truth, "you are God," have more meaning to the student because of his lesson-filled labor? But this poor student doesn't want to recognize the truth. He would rather work in the fields endlessly.

Years ago, when I was a young seeker, I remember asking my Indian yoga teacher how I could know God. My teacher said that my question reminded him of something that had been told to him by his guru, a swami with a long name I no longer remember. It seems that the swami had been approached by one of his students who asked, "How can I know God?"

"How can you know God?" the swami asked. "How can you know God?" he repeated himself. "How can you know God if you don't even know your big toe?" What the swami was asking, of course, was: How can you be aware of God if you're not even aware of the simplest elements of your own being and your own place in the world?

Sometimes when I teach, men and women come up to me during the breaks and ask me how I personally live day to day. They seem to believe that having this information will help them make choices in their own lives. They also ask me what I think they should do about their own personal problems. I honestly believe that if we look clearly at life and at ourselves, we can come up with the answers we need. You can, and I can. Try it. Nobody else can become another person's answer man. Let me clue you in on a little secret, well known to spiritual teachers and wise men the world over: The answers you come up with for yourself regarding your own life are worth more than ten that I or anyone else can provide.

Some people say that the purpose of life is to love and be loved; some say that the purpose of life is to serve God; some say that the purpose of life is the procreation of the race. Buddhism says that the purpose of life is to know oneself, because without that internal self-realization, all other goals will be thwarted. This is the lesson that we all need to learn.

Pain and loss impel us to look inward. Where else can we go? When we know ourselves, we can see reality; when we know ourselves, we can see what is; when we know ourselves, we can find our place in the cosmos. When we fully know ourselves, we will know others. We will be able to comprehend reality and recognize our own inner wisdom, our own divine light, our own Buddha-nature. And we will readily find it in others as well. This realization will transform our lives, our behavior, and our world.

THE WHITE SWAN (HAMSA) MEDITATION

Do you remember that odd quote in biology class about "ontogeny recapitulating phylogeny"? What it refers to is the way an individual event so often recapitulates the larger event that is true to the species as a whole. Mythically speaking, the human race was evicted from paradise, and now all of us individually are trying to return home to find that sense of security and oneness that we have lost. Everyone has intense feelings of separation. When we suffer any kind of loss, it activates our awareness of the larger losses with which we live. What we seek is very much driven by our unconscious feelings of separation and what we are missing. We go through life being compelled to find what we feel we have lost. Our purpose and mission is directing us toward some form of connection or oneness in mystical parlance.

If we here in the post-modern West were to search our human roots for the original story of separation and parting, we would probably arrive at Adam and Eve being torn away from and leaving the Garden of Eden. When this happened they were separated from their spiritual home and their ongoing contact with God. I'm sure they wanted to return. How could they not? And so all of their descendants have longed for a spiritual home as perfect and complete as that lost paradise. The whole spiritual journey is a return home to nonseparation or inseparability, glamorized as heaven, nirvana, or paradise. This is the long, winding trip home to wholeness and completeness.

The spiritual life is about reconnecting with one's inner divinity as well as the divinity of the whole. When we have suffered the loss of love, we tend to feel splattered and scattered. People even say that they feel as though a part of themselves is missing. I once heard a woman say that when her husband died she felt as though she was missing one half of her body.

When we are recovering from loss of any kind, we need to find ways to reconnect with our basic sanity and essential, authentic selves; we need to find kind ways to heal and put ourselves back together again. We need to ground and center ourselves and return home to our innermost being. Chanting mantras, prayer, and meditation practice can be very healing and nurturing. Yoga and spiritual exercise, like physical exercise, is a beautiful way of being good to yourself.

Long before Hinduism and Buddhism, the wise masters of India practiced and transmitted powerful mantras of which the Hamsa meditation is said to be foremost. This timeless wisdom mantra belongs to the ancient Vedic spiritual tradition. The

Vedas are the oldest of man's scriptures, ancient holy texts passed down through the generations. The mantra itself is part of the oral tradition that has continued through these many centuries. Although it is not a Buddhist meditation, it belongs to the Indian yoga tradition that the Buddha himself practiced during the six years of austerity in the wilderness that led up to his enlightenment; I think therefore that it is probably safe to surmise that the Buddha himself used this mantra at some point in his practice.

The mantra itself is deceptively simple. All we need to do is breathe in and out through the nostrils. As we do this we repeat to ourselves the syllable *Ham* on the in-breath, and the syllable *So* on the out-breath.

So simple. So natural. So freeing.

> Repeat on the in-breath: *Ham.*
> On the out-breath: *So*

The syllable *Ham* represents and embodies the expansive masculine yang energy; the syllable *So* represents the centripetal yin, feminine energy.

Hamsa means white swan. The swan, of course, is an ancient symbol of spiritual grace and purity. The mantra is called White Swan because when the in-breath and out-breath are freed and purified, they are like the wings of a swan helping our spirits to soar. The Hamsa mantra helps us find the grace within and carries us beyond our limited concepts. It helps us shed negative feelings that we are ugly ducklings and reminds us that we are all graceful and pure swans. It can help our spiritual lives take wing.

Ancient teachings say this mantra is a vibration of infinite consciousness, uniting us each with the divine source. It is said that this mantra helps us erase duality and the sense that we are different or separate from each other. We cannot find the enlightenment we seek until we realize that we are all one; there is no "other." The Hamsa meditation helps us connect with the divine love and profound energy that flows through the universe and through each of us.

The Hamsa meditation is also known as the "I am that" meditation. This means that the Hamsa meditation gives us an awareness of the connection between the divinity within each of us and the greater infinite divinity. The mantra is also sometimes called the SoHam meditation since it makes little difference which syllable comes first. Once Ramana Maharishi had his disciples contemplating his favorite spiritual practice of questioning and self-inquiry, asking themselves "What Am I?" One of his students, as if in answer, said, "So ham." He said true. So hum! So ha!

When I was given this mantra decades ago by the Hindu Swami Krishnananda at his ashram in Rishikish, I was told that it would help me realize God. I was told to practice it 108 times every morning at dawn. As the light rose, the mantra should arise and spiritual energy would likewise awaken. I found this a great way to practice, there on the Ganges. It works as well here on these shores.

This mantra embodies the ultimate question as well as the answer. It is said that, in each being, the mantra Hamso/Soham continuously throbs and pulsates subconsciously, and that in each twenty-four-hour period the breath or the heart repeats this mantra 21,600 times. It naturally circulates between the throat and forehead chakras as a radiant energy sphere or spiral, which when visualized and breathed completes the cosmic circuit and illuminates all the higher chakras and psychic vortices, awakening us into cosmic consciousness.

We can visualize the mantra written in a circular clockwise fashion around the petals of the lotus-shaped heart chakra, with one syllable inscribed on each petal. Imagine the lotus wheel of the chakras spinning as the mantra turns, spinning off dazzling radiance of light rays and blessings.

We can also use the mantra to "bring down" the blessings

from above, evoking it from the divinity within. We do this by breathing in and saying *Ham* as we visualize light streaming down from the infinite higher power source above the head. Watch it travel down through the crown aperture and instantly descending down the central energy channel into one's heart chakra, making it blaze brightly with light and higher consciousness. Then on the *so,* as we exhale, we visualize all that love and light radiating out from the heart chakra. We do this again and again—*hamsohamsohamsoham*—with light and consciousness coursing through and purifying everything. Indian Vedanta masters teach that the Hamsa mantra is all pervasive and dwells within all beings and all forms, like the ultimate self-nature of the universe.

So let's chant together.

> *Ham* (or *hum*) on the inhalation.
> *So* on the exhalation.

Make the rounds until the in-breath and out-breath and the *ham* and the *so* are all but inseparable. It becomes one constant motion, as if the mantra were written in a circular rather than a linear fashion so that it becomes

Sohamsohamsohamso

Eventually you can't really tell if *Ham* or *So* comes first or second, just as the in-breath and out-breath become fused in the cosmic energy flow, energizing your spiritual nature.

Hamsohamsohamsohamsohamsohamso.

Keep it up.
Enjoy it.
Play with it.
So Hum . . . So Ha . . . so what.
So easy. So free and delight-full.

CHAPTER TWO

Loss and Change

Difficulties are like the ornaments

of a good practitioner.

Dharma is not practiced perfectly

Amidst pleasant circumstances.

DILGO KHYENTSE RINPOCHE

At one time or another everyone loses something. We lose loved ones. We lose our health. We lose our glasses. We lose our memories. We lose our money. We lose our keys. We lose our socks. We lose life itself. We have to come to terms with this reality. Sooner or later, all is lost; we just don't always know when it will happen. Here is a clue: Sherlock Holmes said, "We reach, we grasp, and what is left in our hands in the end? A shadow."

Loss is a fact of life. Impermanence is everywhere we look. All that we gain is eventually lost. Everything that is born withers and dies; the seasons come and go; all of those who are gathered together are eventually parted and scattered. Even great civilizations and empires crumble and return to dust. We are all going to suffer our losses. This is a fact of life. How we deal with these losses is what makes all the difference. For it is not what happens to us that determines our character, our experience, our karma, and our destiny—but how we relate to what happens. This is a key spiritual verity. It helps allow us to take hold of ourselves and our lives. Here opens the way beyond victimhood and on to self-mastery.

Loss is a complex concept. And recovering from loss involves deep and often conflicting emotions. Nobody wants to experience loss. But it's guaranteed that we will. Loss is the elephant in the living room that we all want to ignore or deny. Yet we can't. Some people are so fearful in the face of great loss that they don't want to be around people who are in mourning; some people can't go near hospitals, or cemeteries, or sickrooms. They say that they find it too depressing. They intuitively know that they will not be able to shield themselves indefinitely from life's pain, but even so, they prefer to protect themselves as much as possible. If you don't look, maybe it will go away. Unfortunately, it won't. Life is fraught, fragile, and frangible.

Realistically, since we will all suffer many losses, we need better, more evolved and astute ways of approaching sorrow and emotional pain. We need to be able to be more conscious about the ways our losses can help us become wise and more spiritually evolved; we also need to be more sensitive to and aware of other people's pain and suffering. I have a friend who recently lost her mother. "The worst thing," she told me, "is that I'm embarrassed to cry or express my grief in front of people. I can almost hear people saying, 'What's wrong with her; why can't she get over it? Doesn't she know that she's depressing everybody?'"

Here in this post-modern world, it is not enough to think that we just need to know one strategy for coping with loss and disappointment, for ourselves or for anybody else. In order to recover, grow, and even flourish again, we need to be flexible and resourceful. It's not enough to say, "Let it go," as a Buddhist purist might, or "It's all illusion or maya," as a Hindu might. Helpful as such ancient, timeless, wise aphorisms can be, life is a little more complex than that. We still have to learn how to let go and how to recognize the fleeting illusory nature of our problems and difficulties.

Many men and women from the Christian and Judaic traditions find comfort in thinking, "It's God's will," but even that all-encompassing sentence can't always address the levels of sadness and grief we mere mortals experience when confronted with the anguish of profound loss. Different forms of universal wisdom may tell us to "shake it off," "get over it," "offer it up to God," "learn and grow from it," or that "time heals all wounds," and "what doesn't kill us makes us stronger." We hear people utter words that sound clichéd even when they are true, sentences like

"Every cloud has a silver lining" or "When a door closes, a window opens." To somebody who is suffering from a profound loss, these words can sound superficial and shallow; they can even be infuriating.

But none of this alters the fact that we need to find more enlightened ways of approaching loss. There are so many different modes of suffering and dissatisfaction arising out of the various troubles and travails that afflict us in life. How can we appropriately respond to loss, illness, death, tragedies, failure, calamities, injustice, betrayal, shock, trauma, abuse, grief, and life's most hurtful wounds? Can we do so with wisdom and spirit? These are important questions for those who travel the spiritual path. Let's not shy away from this frightening, yet heartening, fact: Our sorrows provide us with the lessons we most need to learn. Merely diagnosing them all at once and suggesting one strategy like "just move on" is not usually workable, although for some rare individuals such a single formula may sometimes suffice. But for most of us, there are many ways of dealing with loss, just as there are different degrees of loss.

Compare the intensity of losing a tennis game with that of losing a child. Think about the difference between losing a job, a mate, a house, or a parent. Think about what it means to lose innocence, trust, faith, or belief. Some varieties of loss are momentary, while others are more lasting and not necessarily to be swiftly released and forgotten. Some losses, like bankruptcy, unemployment, or eviction, are serious, but they can eventually be put behind us. But others, like the loss of family members, mates, and young children can be so brutal that we may never really get over what we have experienced, nor do we need to. The deep pain we continue to experience reminds us of our love and keeps our hearts open. We discover, often to our amazement and relief, that love is greater than time and place and even greater than death. We discover that we can hold our lost loves in our hearts even as we slowly open to new love.

I began exploring the idea of doing a book on loss from a

Buddhist perspective in the beautiful spring of 2001; that was before the destruction of the World Trade Towers and surrounding events took place. At the time, here in the West at least, the world seemed more innocent and less wracked by pain. Who in this country anticipated that any of us would ever witness such grand-scale loss and suffering? We have all been affected. We all lost.

At 8:45 on the morning of September 11, 2001, my friend Jane was coming out of the Brooklyn Battery Tunnel heading uptown on Manhattan's West Side Highway. She was right alongside the World Trade Center when the first plane collided into the North Tower. She heard a loud explosion-like sound and thought it was an accident involving trucks. Car horns began to honk wildly, and traffic in the opposite direction came to a standstill as the cars tried to turn away from the direction of the crash. Everyone was looking up. She stopped and did the same. That's when she saw smoke pouring out of the gigantic black hole in the tower's wall.

Jane continued driving north staring at the sight in her rear-view mirror for as long as she could. She didn't know what happened, so she turned on the car radio, which was initially reporting that it was a small plane. She began crying for the people inside the tower, but she still didn't know the extent of the tragedy. She remembered reading that a plane had once run into the Empire State Building. She wondered whether this would prove to be the same kind of accident. Jane parked her car at 78th Street and West End Avenue; from there, she could no longer see the World Trade Center. She was so distressed that as she parked her car, she bumped into a brand-new white BMW parked in front of her. The owner of the car was standing next to it. He had a radio to his ear. She got out of her car to apologize and exchange insurance information, but the man waved her away. "It doesn't matter," he said. "It's nothing." He was shaking his head and wiping tears from his eyes. He told her that another plane just rammed into the second tower. Jane didn't know what to do. Like a robot, she continued on to her appointment in a medical office. When she got there, it was apparent that nobody inside had a clue about what was taking place in lower Manhattan. It was business as usual, which brought Jane up short.

"I don't know how to tell you this," Jane announced to the first person she saw. "But the world as we knew it no longer exists. Everything has changed."

So many thousands lost loved ones that day. It hurts just to think about it. So many thousands more lost belongings, homes, and jobs. For all these people, each experiencing different levels and qualities of suffering, everything had changed. For all of us, everything had changed. We lose someone who is precious to us, and our world is never the same. We lose something we hold dear, and our world changes. The world changes moment by moment. In a heartbeat everything changes. You change. I change. We change. Even the atmosphere changes.

With every breath, the old moment is lost; a new moment arrives. This is something Buddhist meditators know. We breathe in and we breathe out. We breathe in and we breathe out. In so doing, we consciously abide in the ever-changing moment. We learn to welcome and accept this entire process.

We exhale, and we let go of the old moment. It is lost to us. In so doing, we let go of the person we used to be. We inhale and breathe in the moment that is becoming. In so doing, we welcome the person we are becoming. We repeat the process. This is meditation. This is renewal. It is also life.

Teachings on the nature of loss and change are the most basic and essential to seekers on the Buddhist path. However, most traditional Buddhist teachers don't call it loss or change; they call it impermanence. Buddhist teachers and teachings remind us time and time again of the spiritual significance of loss and impermanence. They remind us not to run away from our thoughts and feelings about the losses in our lives, but instead to become intimately aware of the gritty facticity of life.

Recently in one of my old notebooks from my days in India, I came across the following instruction from my Tibetan teachers:

> To meditate on impermanence (loss) is to make
> offerings to all the Buddhas.
> To meditate on impermanence is to be rescued
> from suffering by all the Buddhas.
> To meditate on impermanence is to be guided
> by all the Buddhas.
> To meditate on impermanence is to be blessed
> by all the Buddhas.

The meditation on death and impermanence is the king of meditations. Meditating on impermanence is an integral part of the Buddhist path. All the great Tibetan lamas of the past and present have emphasized this practice, advising students not only to meditate on impermanence, but also to do so persistently. This is the tried and true path to transformation and growth. This is the way to enlightenment. The Buddha said that meditating on mortality and impermanence was for him the most important form of contemplation. "Death is my teacher," Buddha said.

Reflect on the instruction "meditate on impermanence," and think about what it means. We meditate on impermanence in order to cultivate a full awareness and appreciation for the transitory nature of life and all things. Nothing ever remains the same; every breath, every moment, every object, every animal, every insect, every bird, every fish, every human is here only for a limited amount of time. When we are going through bad times, it can sometimes be very comforting to be reminded of the fleeting and transitory nature of all things. In short, we are all in the same boat. And it is flowing swiftly downstream. Like a dream.

But good times are also transitory, and who wants to be reminded of that? We want to hang on to the happy and good and let go of the opposite, but we can't get away with that little trick. We don't want to believe that things of beauty and joy will also disappear. And yet, of course, they will.

Everything passes; nothing remains. Understand this, loosen your grip, and find serenity.

SUFFERING, CHANGE, AND LOSS

One of life's hardest lessons is that we can't always protect ourselves or those we love from distressing events. Things keep getting, as the song goes, "all shook up." We think we have everything under control, and then wham! We get clobbered. Sometimes this happens because of mistakes in judgment for which we can easily see how we are personally responsible, but often we don't understand why things have changed for the worse. We don't understand why we keep getting hurt or blindsided by life. We become living examples of the "When Bad Things Happen to Good People" syndrome.

The Buddha taught that suffering and loss are as much a part of living as breathing itself. He said that there are three types of suffering. All are loss-related.

The Suffering of Change

One minute we feel on top of the world; everything is going great; and then somebody lowers the boom. Our lives change. The job, the love, the money, the happy circumstances disappear. If we are fortunate, the losses are primarily material, but often the suffering of change is far more painful. We lose loved ones to death; meaningful relationships split up; good health vanishes; financial security and satisfying jobs are lost; children become alienated and distant. Many of the men and women on medication or visiting therapists' offices are doing so because they are having reactive depressions caused by a loss or change in circumstances. This is the suffering of change.

Suffering upon Suffering

And change upon change. When Heidi recently fell and broke her right leg and had to have a full leg cast, she didn't seem surprised that she had lost mobility for a few months. "Nothing else is going right," she said. "Why should anything change?"

In the last four years, Heidi has faced loss upon loss and suffering upon suffering. Four years ago, the husband she loved started an affair and divorced her to marry somebody else. A year later, Heidi was diagnosed with chronic fatigue syndrome; six months later, her father had a fatal heart attack. Shortly after her father's death, her mother got a rare form of cancer and died within months. Heidi was so distressed from all this that she began losing her hair in clumps.

We all remember the biblical story of Job, who not only lost his oxen, his camels, his sons and his daughters, but was also afflicted with boils. Suffering upon suffering! Change upon change, none of it good. Life is often a matter of suffering upon suffering. Probably the major challenge that we all face is to be able to realistically handle problems and recognize the nature of life without falling into deep despair and depression. Recognizing the universal nature of suffering and that none of us is singled out has brought peace and solace to me in times of despair and tribulation.

I am always impressed by the gentle monk, Thich Nhat Hanh, who lost so many friends, colleagues, and family during the Vietnam War. Because of his Buddhist teachings and outspoken beliefs, he has still not been allowed back into his beleaguered country, where his books are banned and distributed only underground. Nonetheless, he continues to serve as a world renowned teacher and spiritual activist with a shining message of hope and peace. In his lifetime, Thich Nhat Hanh has experienced suffering upon suffering, loss upon loss. Nonetheless, no one can ever meet him, read his words, or see his smiling face

without being inspired. Thay (teacher), as he is called, has made
the glowing hot embers of suffering into a light on his path.

The Suffering and Losses that
Always Surround Us

Look around. Somebody you know is in mourning. Somebody
you know is sad and unhappy. Somebody is ill. Somebody you
know is struggling. Read the newspapers. We are surrounded by
suffering no matter how hard we may try to insulate ourselves
from it. People are hurt; people are scared. So many people are
ill; so many more are living in poverty. Look around in fine
restaurants. See the happy, laughing men and women chowing
down on exquisitely prepared and elegantly presented food. But
even these moments of relaxation are intrinsically connected to
loss. People are eating lobsters that have been plucked from the
sea and boiled alive in a backroom; they are munching on chick-
ens and lambs raised for slaughter—animals that never lived a
normal life in a natural habitat. They are wearing silk clothing
for which millions and millions of silkworms were boiled to
death in steam and destroyed. Even simple vegetarian meals create
suffering. Huge numbers of insects and worms are inevitably killed
in the process of sowing, plowing, pesticiding, and harvesting,

The Buddha taught that no matter where we are, or what we
are doing, we are surrounded by loss and suffering. There is no
escaping it. This is the bad news. The good news is that it is a
universal reality; it is not your fault or your punishment. Nor
will it persist forever. Remember the vital, liberating Buddhist
mantra, "This too shall pass."

This thought continues to free me.

UNRELENTINGLY GLOOMY OR
APPROPRIATELY REALISTIC

Does all this talk about suffering and loss seem depressing? Do you wish that I would change the subject? That's what most of us have been trained and conditioned to do. Instead of dealing with the reality of loss, we crank up the music, have a munch or a drink, pick up the phone and try to insulate ourselves from pain. Rather than feeling our feelings, we try to lose ourselves in habitual activity. Sometimes we drink, smoke, or take drugs. Sometimes our denial mechanisms are so sophisticated that we are easily able to blot out the reality of what we are experiencing. Of course it's a terrible thing to be in any kind of pain, but when we run from the truth of what we are experiencing, all we are doing is digging deeper ruts. We are doing the opposite of seeking truth; rather, we are running and hiding from it.

It goes without saying that while there are people who are shockingly adept at avoiding their true feelings, there are others who seem to find excess solace in experiencing every bit of pain. The teachings of the Buddha stress balance. There is always a danger of getting stuck and wallowing in discomfort, and we have to watch ourselves so that we don't become long-suffering victims. Buddhism teaches us to look at our losses realistically; it teaches us to feel what we feel and experience what we experience. Buddha Dharma instructs us in how to unflinchingly cultivate clear vision and to fully inhabit our present experience. It also teaches us the wisdom of releasing the pain and allowing ourselves to be nourished by life. The Buddha also taught what he called "wise avoidance."

A oft-quoted story about the Buddha revolves around his early years on the spiritual path. Mendicant yogis of the time devoted themselves one hundred percent to meditation and extreme ascetic practices. The Buddha did likewise, fasting for weeks at a time. Finally, he was so weakened that he was literally at death's door. He was so physically emaciated and weak that he almost drowned while washing in a river. A kind young woman who fed him a bowl of sweetened rice curd is credited with providing the nourishment that saved his life. Some of his fellow seekers were disturbed that he gave up life-threatening asceticism and fasting, and they left him. The Buddha, however, was a remarkably practical man. When he recovered, he thought about the extremes of asceticism and decided that it wasn't effective, necessary, or wholesome.

In my mind's eye, I can see the Buddha weakened and near death, shaking his head and saying, "This is crazy; there's got to be a better way." The Buddha recognized that going overboard in any direction, whether it be hedonism or asceticism, was counterproductive to a sane and well-rounded spiritual path. Throughout his life, he taught his followers to value balance, restraint, and moderation. He called it the Middle Way: a path of harmonious, nonharming moderation, virtue, and spiritual investigation—a practical application of the Golden Mean.

Reflection on Impermanence

Whatever prepares you for death enhances life.

STEPHEN LEVINE

Sit someplace where you can be quiet and alone. Try to find a place that brings you closer in touch with a sense of the natural ebb and flow of all life. In Tibet, this kind of meditation is often done outdoors in a cemetery, or beneath clouds moving across the sky, but these particular forms aren't absolutely necessary. You can watch the waves move in and out on a beach; you can sit near a waterfall or in a park. In autumn you can watch leaves flutter to the ground. Other places sometimes suggested to increase awareness of impermanence would be the city dump, car junkyard, or hospital entrance.

Wherever you are, get comfortable. Release the muscular tension throughout your body. Breathe in through your nostrils; breathe out through your nostrils. Do this several times until you are feeling relaxed and settled.

Rest in the moment. Stay with this awareness of breathing. Be aware, attentive, and mindful. Feel what you feel and sense what you sense in the immediacy of the present experience. Breathe in through your nostrils. And then breathe out. And go through this cycle again and again.

Let your breaths come and go, rise and fall, like waves in the sea and clouds in the infinite sky. Again and again . . . like gently rhythmic waves.

Notice whatever comes to mind. Simply be with what you are presently experiencing, beyond judgment and beyond interference or alteration. Don't suppress what you feel or what you think. But also don't allow your mind to get carried away into trains of discursive thinking. For the moment, don't try to work or figure anything out. Just be mindfully aware of whatever appears for you in the field of consciousness. Stay with breath-awareness; observe the breath flowing in and out of your nostrils. Pay attention.

When you are calm, still, and centered, reflect on the changing nature of the seasons in the places where you have lived and visited. Remember how they have flowed one into another, one season giving way to the next. Reflect on the heavy snowstorms, chilly winter days, and icy streets; reflect on the melting snow as spring arrives with its crocuses, daffodils, and tulips; reflect on rising temperatures and how spring becomes summer; reflect on long hot summer days; reflect on the coming of autumn with the changing leaves and shortening days and the return of arctic air.

Reflect on the changing nature of the globe, its geological formation and the aeons and eras of change; reflect on the disappearance of the gigantic dinosaurs who once walked the earth, the advent of man, the rise and fall of language, civilization, religions, cultures, and countries.

Reflect on the great saints and sages of history, how they lived and died, and what they left behind.

Reflect on the various great world civilizations and their rise and fall over centuries.

Reflect on what has happened in your own country during your own lifetime. Reflect on the elections and political leaders who have been part of your world. Reflect on how their views and times created changes.

Reflect on the major national and world events during your own lifetime and how important everything seemed at the time it happened. Reflect on how dreamlike and fleeting it all is.

Reflect on the various sporting events, sporting figures, and competitions that have been important to you. Reflect on the sports figures who have retired, grown old, or stopped competing.

Reflect on the powerful, rich, and glamorous celebrities you've seen featured in magazines and newspapers during your lifetime. Reflect on how fame and reputations ebb, wane, and fade. Reflect on how ephemeral it all is.

Reflect on the economy and the stock market with its various changes and surprises, ups and downs, over the past year, over the decades of your life, and over the past hundred years.

Continue breathing in and out through your nostrils. Rest in the ever-present present moment, without letting your attention stray.

Embrace your reflections with awareness, accepting everything as it is without judgment or any need to work things out. For the moment, just stay with the awareness component of this meditative reflection.

Let it all settle, dissolve, return back to where it all arose. Just sit and breathe. Relax and smile. Abide in the moment with nothing more to do, figure out, or achieve.

Let it all be, as it is. Love it and leave it, with a light, lovely touch. Let things fall as they may.

Everything is perfectly in place. Rest your weary heart and mind, and replenish your energy at the cosmic fountain of natural breath and natural mind.

> *In pursuit of the world,*
> *One gains more and more.*
> *In the pursuit of the Tao, one gains less and less.*
> *Loss upon loss until at last comes rest.*
> *When nothing is done, nothing remains undone.*

> LAO TZU,
> *Tao Te Ching*

CHAPTER THREE

Naming Our Losses

Nothing that grieves us can be called little: by the eternal laws of proportion a child's loss of a doll and a king's loss of a crown are events of the same size.

MARK TWAIN

In much of India, tattered, homeless beggars abound. Many live under bridges or manage to find temporary shelter from the harsh elements under the eaves of bus and train stations and near roadside water spigots and latrines. Some years back, when I was a young man, still in my twenties, I used to travel through India on rickety buses on which you could go hundreds of miles for about a quarter. One day I got off an Indian train in Mathura Station, near the Taj Mahal. It was dusk, and I saw a group of children begging. One of them was a young boy with elephantiasis. He couldn't have been much more than ten, and he was draped in a burlap-sack shawl. The boy hobbled up to me, asking for baksheesh, alms. He was wobbling; one of his feet was the size of a football. He had large eyes, and he looked as though he was starving. I was so stunned and moved by his appearance that I didn't know what to do. I gave him a handful of rupees, brutally aware of the insignificance of my gift. The boy was all excited as he hurried back to the other children. His expectations from life were so minimal that he could be made happy by a few miserable paper notes.

The boy was living on the street, so he had probably lost his parents. His physical appearance attested to the fact that he had lost his health. His eyes told me that he had already lost hope. His plight was so severe, and there was little or nothing that I could do. He was so young, and yet he had lost so much. Even so, he could still be overjoyed, however briefly. My heart broke at the sight.

I am generally a hardened case when it comes to feelings. Not unlike many men of my generation and probably others too, I have learned to protect and insulate that tender spot at the heart of each of us, which is so vulnerable to grief, loss, and sorrow. But when I saw that little boy, I started to cry at the enormity of his situation, and that of all the other deprived children. As an American who had never been deprived, it gave me a sense of perspective. It was this child's gift to me, and unlike the few rupees I handed him, it was a significant gift.

Here in the West, we are rarely prepared for this scale of loss. We take a certain level of creature comfort very much for granted. When we watch news clips of impoverished children in other countries, we are sad, but it seems far away. We watch television commercials, sitcoms, and glamorous films, and we anticipate beautiful, exhilarating, sun-drenched, healthy lives filled with joy and love. After all, we are the heroes and heroines, the "good guys" of our own lives. Don't the good guys always end up getting "the good stuff"? Good guys aren't supposed to lose. Unlike the child in India, we are raised to have high expectations. For some of us, the most consistently troublesome thing about loss is the destruction of expectations.

Many of us are uncomfortable around loss; when things go wrong in our lives, we are sometimes surprised to discover that we feel and act almost embarrassed, as though we had something to be ashamed of. We have been told too many times that "everybody loves a winner" and "nobody loves a loser." And yet, of course, we know realistically that even "winners" suffer great loss.

The tendency to hide loss and bury it under the carpet, so to speak, is understandable. Not that long ago I was introduced to a man at a party. He had just recently lost a good job, and people were asking about it. I could tell that he was trying to put his loss in a good light. "Probably the best thing that ever happened to me," he said. He reassured everyone that he was in good shape financially and that he had "many prospects" lined up. He adamantly denied that he felt scared and worried.

Another friend of mine recently lost an upper-management job, and as part of the severance "package" from her previous employer she was given several weeks of counseling with an out-placement firm that specializes in helping people find new jobs. In her first week there, she went to a group counseling session with about fifteen other men and women who were discussing what had happened to them. She said she was shocked and sur-prised at the level of anger and hurt that she felt. It was comfort-ing and reassuring to be with a group of people with whom she could openly share her feelings of having been wrongfully and heartlessly fired or downsized.

She told me that at the beginning of the session everyone there was putting a good face on the loss of employment. Two hours later, the group was being much more honest with them-selves and others. They all began to admit to feelings of anger, hurt, and fear. One man began to cry and thanked the group for helping him open up. He said that he was so taken aback when he was fired, after ten years of employment, that he was in shock and couldn't acknowledge the magnitude of his loss. He told the group that he had been a workaholic who had given this job all of his time and creative energy. Now he felt like a fool. He said that acknowledging the depth of his loss and talking about it to a group of supportive peers was a turning point in his healing process.

When bad things happen, we want to stay honest with our-selves about our feelings. We don't want to lose our capacity to feel; we don't want to become so hardened and frozen that we can't experience or remember the negative things that happened to us. Repressing difficult experiences and feelings can make us ill. Acknowledging our pain is a necessary part of our healing.

Examining our lives and losses for deeper meaning is an important part of being on a spiritual path. Yet loss and suffering can also bring faith. Suffering can be redemptive; it helps burn away superficiality and complacency. Buddha said that suffering is the proximate cause for the arising of faith and compassion.

Do you ever think about the losses in your life? I know I do. Here are some of the people, ideas, beliefs, and things I've lost in the course of my lifetime. I lost my beloved grandmas and grandpas, favorite aunt and uncles; my sixteen-year-old friend, Jay, who died on a motorcycle; my friend Alison, who was killed in 1971 at Kent State when she was nineteen. I've lost too many precious enlightened gurus and teachers to whom I was close. The list seems endless. Just this year, as I was working on this book, I lost my beautiful white sheep dog, Chandi, who became ill and died.

I've lost energy, time, memory, patience, and the mental acuity of youth. I've lost innocence, opportunities, and naiveté, along with virginity a long time ago. I've lost friends, family, neighbors, and neighborhoods I loved. I've lost the athletic ability of a teenage jock. I've lost apartments, homes, jobs, and girlfriends.

I've lost connections to trains, planes, busses, and, yes, people. I've lost old picture albums, favorite books, watches, rings, bathing suits, good clothes, keys, phone numbers, and a three-speed bike that was stolen.

I've lost track of my purpose more than a few times. Fortunately, I lost the adolescent belief that I knew more than anybody else did. I also lost the belief that the sixties' countercultural perspective could and would change the world. I lost my fear of commitment. Somewhere along the line I also lost my fear of getting old. And I lost my absolutist belief that there are idealized solutions for all problems and that perfect choices can be found and made.

Unquestionably, the biggest loss for me was my father's death. I sometimes ask myself why I was so saddened by this. The answer comes immediately: He was my only father; he was my dad. That fact goes far deeper than words and concepts. I miss him in many ways, although I often feel as though he is with me and that he is still living there in peaceful retirement on Long

Island while I'm wandering around the world. He's only been dead for six years, and perhaps I haven't gone through enough of the grieving process to really accept and know that he's gone. He gave me so much; maybe that's why I feel as though he's still here. He gave me the best of himself, which remains with me.

I was well fathered. I never felt like an orphan or somebody who was gypped of parental love. Whatever there is between fathers and sons, he passed it on to me. He was always there for me, so much so that I took it for granted. To me, my father right now is most conspicuous by his absence at family events, like Thanksgiving, Passover, and other holidays and celebrations, like when my brother's daughter was born. That's when Dad is really supposed to be there, according to the laws of my personal world, and achingly isn't.

So much changed in my family when my father died, particularly for my mother, who had been "Harold's wife" for forty-eight years. My parents married the day after my mother graduated from college; my mother is still living in the suburban corner house she and my father bought in 1955. Unfortunately, my parents had resisted the tides of change for so long that when my father died, Mom felt it was too late for her to move. She has had such a hard time dealing with this huge, traumatic change and loss, which reverberates strongly in everything she does in an almost paralyzing, terrifying way. Like many widows and widowers, she struggles with loneliness. Making peace with her new identity and the shifts in how she is perceived by others is challenging. As she has told me on several occasions with great sadness, "Jeffrey, no one is still alive who remembers me as I was."

What did I learn from my father's death and the changes that surrounded it? I learned how huge he was in my life and how I had hardly even noticed that fact during his lifetime because he was so "there." It was like a fish hearing the word *water* and not knowing what it means. Being alone with him in his hospital room early one morning as he breathed his last in his sleep and sitting with him for forty-five minutes afterward until a nurse came to check on him was a powerful experience. It was a meaningful way to be with my father even as he was dead. I felt it was a blessing to be with him then and there, as he was always there for me—as he had always been at my bedside whenever I was in a hospital, and as he was always at the airport when I came and went. Love means being there. That was what he taught me.

For me the moment of greatest loss came as they put his body into a grave. It was a visceral tug, and I felt the loss on a cellular level. He was being torn away. I learned at that precise moment that I had powerful feelings that I had never fully appreciated. The whole experience also showed me that if you don't face change, you miss the opportunity to extract, digest, and internalize the lessons connected to it.

I've asked various people to tell me about the greatest losses in their lives. Here are some of the answers I've received. As you read this, think about the story of the Buddha and the bereaved mother who went from house to house trying to find a home that had not been touched by loss. Think about the stories she must have heard.

Laura's Losses

The overriding loss in my life is a sense of not having a family and roots, even though many members of my family are alive and well. I grew up with a self-involved father, a brother who has always been in denial, and an inconsistent mother who had a heart attack and died when she was much too young. My feelings of familial loss crystallized for me when my parents separated and decided to get a divorce. I had just left our comfortable home in the suburbs and gone off to college, and when I wanted to come home for the holidays, there was no home for me to return to. My mother had moved into a tiny studio apartment and my father had rented out my room. I should make it clear that my father is a successful professional who has two homes, and we lived in an environment where there was an expectation of parental roles.

I often feel as if I have no real sense of security and no place to go. This, in turn, makes me anxious, uncomfortable, and worried. These feelings intensified when I was in my early twenties, and my mother died suddenly. Many of my friends have strong security nets to fall back on when anything goes wrong. I don't. This makes me feel depressed and sometimes angry, particularly at my father, who, to say the least, is not a very protective or nurturing dad. Again, I should state that I wouldn't feel this way if my father was poor or financially strapped. He has never helped me, and if I were really in trouble, I can pretty much guarantee from experience that my father wouldn't respond positively.

I feel as though I am always trying to make up for this lack. I spend a lot of time trying to establish a sense of security on my own, but it's not really the same. Also, I've worked very hard at establishing strong friendships to take the place of family connections. For reasons I don't fully understand, I think I still have the expectation that my father will one day become a better parent. This expectation is probably fed by what I see around me. Many of the people I know have doting parents. I try not to envy them. I try to work with my expectations. And I try to create a life filled with the kind of loving friendship that will help me compensate for what I didn't have. I once read that forgiveness means letting go of the hope for a better past.

Frank's Losses

My father died when I was seventeen. My mother fell apart and couldn't really deal with anything, including me. I don't blame her; she was a wreck. I ended up going to my best friend Joe's house for dinner every night. His family helped me out so much. Then Joe's parents died within a year of each other when we were both in our mid-twenties. A couple of years ago, my friend Joe was diagnosed with leukemia. He died six months ago. At the end, he lived with me and my wife. He was very close to my kids. In the months before his death, he needed a lot of help. He was such a good guy. I'm really having a hard time with his death. I guess I should be embarrassed about all the crying I do, but I'm not. I miss my friend so much. It's rare to have a friend like him.

Pam's Losses

My dog died in April, my mother died in May, and then in June my boyfriend told me that he was in love with somebody else. The only reason why I was able to get through this was that I had a new job that I loved. Then in September, my boss called me in and told me that there were going to be huge budget cuts, and he had no choice but to let me go. He didn't give me a reason, and when I asked for one, he told me to talk to Human Resources. The head of Human Resources told me that she didn't have any idea why I was being let go. In fact, she seemed surprised and a little angry that my boss had passed the buck to her. I had no idea my job was in jeopardy; only the week before, I brought in a huge contract and had been told how well I was doing.

I have been having an impossible time getting over my anger and hurt over the job loss. After I left, my boss took credit for all the business that I brought in and then he hired his girlfriend to service the accounts. My rage at the unfairness of what happened to me is overwhelming. All of this coincided with fighting in the Middle East, which also upset me terribly because I have family in Israel. Almost every night I have nightmares in which terrorists run around dropping bombs. Some nights they look like Osama Bin Laden; other times they look like my ex-boss. I keep telling myself that it was just a job, but it was an exciting job with a lot of status and prestige, and there isn't another one like it anywhere near here. I've been out of work for over six months, and I still haven't told all of my friends. I'm still too upset to talk about it. I feel depressed and discouraged. I tell myself that I shouldn't feel humiliated, but I do because I had been so proud of getting the job and my achievements there that I told everybody. Now I look like a complete fool. I'm running out of money, and I'm worried about being evicted. Even so, I don't have the energy or the will to go job hunting. I need to let go of my misfortune and move on; I should start talking to people in my field about finding work, but I still feel too sad.

Molly's Losses

I have two losses that compete as to which is the biggest. The first is my mother's death. She was the one person in the world who gave me a sense of unconditional love. I talked to her daily and shared everything with her. After she became ill, she lived with me for almost a year. She was very sick and taking care of her was extraordinarily difficult. I hated it and felt miserable at the time. Nonetheless, when she died, I was stunned by how much I missed her. I realized that I would much rather take care of somebody I love, no matter how hard it is, than lose that person.

The second is the end of a love relationship with a man who I trusted totally. We had been together for a long time, and he always told me that I was the love of his life. When he split up with me, I had no idea it was coming. I lost him, but I also lost something bigger: I lost my sense of hope and a belief in love. I also lost the capacity to trust. This is a lot to lose. I sometimes feel that since he was the person who took away that trust, he is the only person who can give it back, which I know is foolish, but that's how I often feel.

Sam's Losses

I've had a lot of losses in my life: a father, who abandoned us when I was still a baby; my grandmother, who was raising me, died when I was in my teens. I've lost just about all my relatives, as well as too many close friends, to death, people who died from cancer, heart attacks, and accidents. And I've had my heart broken more times than I care to count. My separation from my wife and kids was very tough to handle. However, the events of the past few years, beginning with September 11, are the worst things that ever happened to me, and I wasn't even directly affected. The twin towers, the wars, the bombings, and the pain in the world—it's hard to even think about.

What I lost is a kind of fearlessness and a faith that no matter what, everything would turn out okay. I can no longer feel that way. It made me realize how fortunate I was to feel protected and safe for most of my life, although I had overlooked that sense of security at the time. I used to feel bitter and angry about not being with my children every night. Now I just feel grateful that nothing happened to them. I try to remember to enjoy what we have instead of crying over what used to be.

Matt's Losses

My older brother died before I was born, and that kind of impacted very heavily on my parents. They must have been afraid of losing me too because they really did spoil me. Nothing serious went wrong in my life until last year, when I lost my job and all my money. That changed everything. I got kicked pretty bad by the failure of the dot-coms. I'm only thirty-six, but even so I feel like a has-been. I was really doing well and making a lot of money. I had just bought a condo, I had a good car, and my girlfriend and I were planning a big wedding. That's when the bottom fell out. One day I was congratulating myself on how smart I had been; the next I felt like a total ass for believing that the market was going to continue going up. Did I tell you that I also worked on Wall Street? Not only did I lose my money, I lost my job.

I have two children from an early marriage. I had the money so I didn't mind giving my ex-wife whatever she needed for my kids. But she doesn't seem to believe that I don't have it anymore. I'm not even sure if my kids do. When the bottom fell out for me, my girlfriend—now my wife—and I went through with the wedding, but it was very scaled back. We had planned to get married in Hawaii, and I was going to fly my family and hers out for the ceremony. Instead we were married in our local Botanical Gardens with a small reception. It was nice, but I think my wife felt disappointed. In the meantime, my son and daughter seem to blame my new wife for the fact that we had to put them back in public school. This has been rough on my wife, who really wants to have a good relationship with my kids. She's been a real doll about all this, but then we had another blow. Her only child, a daughter who is living with us, was diagnosed with a serious illness that requires a great deal of medical attention. They think she will be okay, but it's no picnic.

I got so depressed that I went on medication. Everything that happened this year seemed designed to make me grow up. I was lucky because I got another job, but I can't help thinking about all the money I lost and how I think money would cure most of my problems. I didn't expect any of this to happen and I wasn't prepared. Right now I still feel angry at everybody and scared about what might happen next. I know it's sick, but that's the way it is.

Jamie's Losses

Jamie is seven years old. He is a beautiful, talented, bright, open-hearted child with a powerfully sweet smile. He is one of two children in an upper-middle-class family in Manhattan. Both of his parents are highly educated and successful professionals. He was born when his older brother was five, and both his parents took a lot of time off to spend with both children. When he was an infant, Jamie's mother took him to her office or came home from work in order to maintain his feeding schedule. Jamie's father has always been very involved in child care. When Jamie's parents were at work, either a loving nanny or his maternal grandmother cared for him. Jamie's brother is an extremely kind, good-natured child who was loving to his baby brother.

Jamie and his brother are much-adored children. They go to good schools; they have a house full of toys and books; they play team sports and have music lessons. They have friends and play-dates and sleepovers. Many of their weekends are spent at the family's house in the country, where the two boys swim in the summer and ski in the winter. Jamie's parents would do anything to protect their children. When Jamie was four, he lost one of his grandparents; shortly thereafter, a grandmother was diagnosed with Alzheimer's. Soon after that, the grandmother who baby-sat died suddenly. Jamie really missed his grandma. He asked his mother, "If everybody in the world stood on top of each other's shoulders, and if they put me up on the very top, would I be able to see my grandma?"

A few months after his grandmother's death, Jamie's father was diagnosed with a serious life-threatening illness. Both Jamie's mother and father threw themselves into the business of trying to deal with and cure what was diagnosed as an incurable disease. The whole house was turned topsy-turvy with both parents racing to doctors and health practitioners. They both tried to keep things balanced for their children, but the stress and worry they felt couldn't help but spill over to their children. Jamie asked, "Is Daddy going to die?" "Don't be stupid," his older brother responded at first, "of course he's not going to die." Then the boy looked at his mother. "Is he?" he asked.

Jamie and his family lived a few blocks from the World Trade Center. Jamie's mother took him to school on the morning of September 11 and was there talking with his teacher when the first plane hit the World Trade Center. From the windows of Jamie's school, the children could see everything that was happening. They saw the smoke; they saw the people jumping from the top. One of the children was the first to notice what was happening. "The birds are on fire," the child screamed.

Fortunately, all of the children were led to safety amid the chaos and terror. Jamie's family could not return home to their apartment for months because it was filled with ash and dust, and the smell was unbearable. Jamie is still so young that it's hard for his parents to know how he has been shaped by his experiences.

WHAT ARE YOUR GREATEST LOSSES?

Naming our losses helps keep us conscious of them. It helps us appropriately process our lives and stay in touch with our own inner core.

It stands to reason that in order to know ourselves we have to be aware and conscious of those things that have touched us deeply. We have to experience our pain and realistically process our losses. The path to enlightenment is the path of becoming more fully awake and conscious.

Jung said, "The psychological rule says that when an inner situation is not made conscious, it happens outside as fate." Buddhism says something very similar. It reminds us that if we don't learn from our history, then karmic conditioning dictates that we will keep reproducing similar situations. The kind of higher education we gain through spiritual learning develops as we face the truth, the reality of the happenings of our lives.

Thoreau was fond of quoting Socrates, who said that the unexamined life is not worth living. This belief in the value of reflection and self-examination is one of the roots of the American Transcendental movement. True introspection and self-examination can be painful, particularly if one is already dealing with one of life's little body blows. But we can't afford to bury our pain and go into denial. Sadness and sorrow is part of the truth of life.

On the other hand, of course, we also don't want to hang on to our pain and suffer even more by wallowing in it. The Buddha advised his followers to stay present in the immediacy of the moment and to acknowledge and feel whatever it is that arises or appears. Staying centered in the moment without hanging on to the past or fantasizing about the future is one of the greatest challenges on the spiritual path.

Using a Journal to Help Process Our Losses

Many of us are so quick to deny and cover up the true roots of our unhappiness that we are unaware of the depths of our buried suffering. We lose track of the patterns that haunt us, and we fail to find meaning and purpose in our experience. We get mired in our guilt or anxiety; we get overwhelmed by our sadness. Writing about your losses in a journal is not about getting stuck in the past. It's not about dredging up all the painful garbage and then getting stuck in your misery. The teachings of the Buddha about staying in the present moment remind us that we don't want to get mired in our pain. We do, however, want to bring any painful, orphaned feelings and thoughts into the light of conscious awareness so that we can deal with them intelligently and sensitively and thus find some healing and closure.

It's difficult to stay conscious and current—up to date with the inner life—when we are carrying around a lifetime worth of raw losses that haven't been processed. I personally have found journal writing to be a very healthy and healing way of bringing hidden or unconscious feelings and emotions to the surface. Then it becomes easier to identify and relinquish those negative emotions, habits, and behaviors that are keeping us stuck. Remember that the first step in recovery from any loss is acknowledging what we have experienced.

The first thing you need in order to chronicle your losses is a journal. Buy a notebook specifically for this purpose. Try to find one that is a little different from those you usually buy. Choose a different color, size, or design. This is a way of getting out of habitual ruts. Find a good time each day to work in your journal. Before you get started, take a few moments to get centered. Give yourself the gift of some calm reflection. Breathe in and out through your nostrils, relax your body, center yourself, and allow yourself to settle and quiet down. Tune in to your inner self.

Start listing your greatest losses from the top of the page down. Just jot down whatever comes to mind. This is not a test; nothing has to be alphabetized. Skim the surface at first, and just see what comes up. Don't worry about whether or not you are writing exquisite prose. In some ways journal writing in this way corresponds with the tantric principle of getting it all out until you are exhausted and then seeing who you are at the bedrock level. Some people are working through a current loss; others are enmeshed and caught up in the past. Start from wherever you are.

After you have skimmed the surface, you might want to consolidate your loss list or break it down into categories such as "material loss," "relationship loss," "lost opportunities," or "lost dreams," to name just a few possibilities. Which areas stand out for you? A friend told me that for her it all comes down to lost love and fears of loneliness. Others say they are most aware of squandered opportunities and accompanying feelings of self-recrimination. Some are traumatized most by world events. Still others are focused on health issues.

With each of your losses, reflect on what happened. Reflect on your deepest feelings and get into the details. When you start writing, you might be surprised at the losses that take priority. One person told me that he expected his greatest loss to be the breakup of a relationship that happened only a few months ago, but when he started writing he realized that his most important feelings around loss were centered on the death of his grandmother when he was a teenager. This loss, which he never fully acknowledged or worked through, has colored his entire life.

With each loss that you write down, ask yourself the following question: What did I really lose? List the answers and work them through. For example, if you lost your job, and one of your losses is a sense of status, ask: "Is this really important to me? And why?"

Here are some suggestions for questions to get you started.

~ What did I really lose?
~ Why did I lose it?
~ Have I healed from this loss?
~ Will I ever heal from this loss?
~ Do I want to heal from this loss?
~ If I have healed, what lessons have I learned about myself?
~ What lessons can I apply to current or future loss?
~ Have I stopped blaming myself?
~ What can I do to be more accepting and forgiving of my own behavior?

Name and write down the feelings you are experiencing.

Somerset Maugham once said that if he wanted to get over something he had to write about it. Every loss leaves us with feelings and emotions that need processing. Use your journal to write down what you are feeling because of your loss. Which feelings are you having a difficult time releasing? Ask yourself:

~ Am I still angry and bitter?
~ Why am I still hanging on to losses that have no real meaning in my life?
~ Am I hanging on to unrealistic fantasies and illusions around my loss? (For example: Do I believe that my ex-partner will someday return?)
~ How can I let go of my negative feelings?

Remember that writing is as cathartic as it is creative. Often when we have lost something, we blame ourselves. We think, If I had turned left instead of right, the situation might have had a different outcome. People blame themselves if their partners cheat or their children become ill, but it isn't spiritually intelligent to blame ourselves. There are many factors involved with each event, and we can't control the ungovernable world. Getting more in touch with your feelings about the major, and minor, losses in your life can help you heal and forgive yourself. This can be an important first step on the road back to wholeness.

CHAPTER FOUR

Letting Go of
the Person You
Used to Be

"Great teacher," said Upashiva, "when one is free from attachment and craving, when everything is let go and one depends on emptiness, will one be permanently in that state?"

"When you are free from craving for sense pleasures and when you are aware of emptiness, you are free in a supreme way and that will not change. It is like a flame struck by a gust of wind. In a flash the flame has gone out. Similarly, the person is suddenly free and no more words can be said. When all the ways of being a self are let go and when all phenomena are seen to be empty, then all the ways of describing this have also vanished."

GUTTA NIPATA,

from *Buddha Speaks*,

ed. Anne Bancroft

Sometimes in the middle of the night, I think about the person I used to be. I think about my previous lives within this lifetime—about my college years in Buffalo, New York, and the time I spent in Tibetan monasteries. I think about the people I loved and cared about, people who I no longer see. I wonder where they have gone and what they are doing. I think about people who are no longer in this world, and I wonder about them as well. Some mornings as I get out of bed, I wonder about what happened to me, the teenager who got up early Saturday morning to read a book before rushing off to baseball practice at 8 A.M. I remember how secure my life felt when I was living at home back in the fifties with healthy young parents and my sister and brother. I remember how I felt when I was living on a Darjeeling hilltop listening to the teachings of a wise old lama in the shadow of the lofty snowpeaks. All of this seems like a magical dream to me today, real as it was at the time, and I am reminded of Buddha's own words: "See this floating world as like a dream, like a mirage, like a fantasy."

I also remember all the firm opinions I held at various times in my life. Growing up, I didn't understand why everybody didn't view everything the same way I did, in accordance with the beliefs of my middle-class, suburban New York, Jewish family. I remember the time long ago when I thought girls were a foreign species and that I would never want or be able to talk to them about any of the things that mattered. I remember my utter shock in sixth grade when I went to a dance party and became involved with my first girlfriend and discovered that we did, indeed, have some things in common. Suddenly it was as if I were in a new life, a different incarnation in the land of teens.

I remember a time long ago when I thought I would never want to live anywhere except New York, and a time when I honestly believed my entire future hinged on the outcome of a chemistry exam, and a time when I thought I would spend my life in a monastery. I remember when I could eat anything I wanted without gaining weight or a percentage point of cholesterol. I remember when my blood pressure was always steady, and I could play at athletics all day without a single cramp, strain, or sprain. How long ago was that! Whose body did I inhabit at that time, so different from mine now?

I remember how I felt when I first fell in love as a teenager, and how I felt when the love suddenly evaporated. I also remember friends, relatives, and teachers who died and left me without their supportive physical presence and loving connections. All these changes meant that my world had changed, and that therefore I had changed as well.

I resist and hate change as much as the next guy. I'm still trying to wear my cutoff blue jeans and rainbow shirt. Much to my wife's dismay, disgust even, I hang on to an old windbreaker from Members Only that my father gave me when I was twenty-five years younger and a few sizes smaller. I have only recently been forced to retire some pink and purple shirts, leather vests, and other vestigial, psychedelic remnants and relics of the sixties. What is really hard is letting go of those well-worn, comfy shoes and sweaters, even if they look like absolute hell. They feel so good. I guess I'm attached to them. The clothes closets of the world would all breathe a sigh of relief if we could all learn some of those little lessons. We too would breathe easier if our personal space—outer and inner—became uncluttered.

Pens and pencils, files and notepads represent other little attachments that I form. Useless pens haunt my desk and writing areas. Why can't I let them go into the wastebasket where they belong? I must have missed that lesson in school. I still have a wooden twelve-inch ruler with three holes that fit neatly into my high school looseleaf binder. Do I believe that it will return to an earlier functionality here in the digital age where I'm using a laptop computer? Why do I resist recycling or discarding clothes that I hardly ever wear or that are just plain tattered? Do I hope that I will someday be able to once again wear them? Do I cling to them because I cling to the memories they represent? Do I await someone to pass them on to, like a priceless spiritual transmission? When I look at my old India cotton shirts in the closet, I remember the times and places I wore them. If I discard them, will I lose touch with the memories? Will I throw out an important part of who I am? Who will I be if I am rid of all my stuff?

My friend Sarah is living in a house that is much too big and costly for her to manage now that her children are grown. If she moved someplace smaller, she would be less financially stressed; she could cut back the number of hours she works. Sarah knows that she should move, and she says she wants to move, but she says the primary reason why she stays there is that she doesn't know what to do about her books. Throughout her life, Sarah has never recycled any books or magazines. She has shelves and shelves of old tattered and torn mysteries, for example. She has no plans to read any of them again. Nonetheless, each one of them tells her a story, and it's not about the author's fiction. "See this mystery," she says. "I think it was terrible, and I don't remember the plot. What I do remember is reading it lying on the couch in front of the fire while a blizzard stormed out doors. I was so cozy and happy. I didn't even get out of my flannel pajamas that day. Halfway through the book, the dog needed to go out. I remember putting on all my outdoor clothes and boots over my pajamas, and the dog and I tried to take a walk. We didn't get much farther than the end of the driveway, but it was snowing so hard that both the dog and I had a hard time getting back to the door. In front of the door, he was covered with so much snow that I couldn't even see his face. He didn't shake himself off until he got back inside and then it was like a cartoon creature. He was so funny. That sweet dog has since died, but when I see that book on my shelves, that's what I remember about it. How can I throw it away?

"Sometimes I try to discard books. I take a stack and put them in the hall so that I can donate or discard them. Then I look at the spaces in the bookcase where the books used to be and I get scared. I can't let go of them. So I trudge down the hall and bring them back. Even when they can't be read because they are falling apart, I hang on."

We can certainly all sympathize with Sarah's memories of her beloved dog and her tendency to treasure her belongings as well as her loving associations. But it's easy to see that Sarah's need to hang on to dusty books symbolizes her reluctance to change and move on with her life. Maybe she would be better off with a new way of life in harmony with who she is now.

We are all connected to people, places, things, traditions, beliefs, habits, and ideas. To some degree, we tend to define ourselves by these connections. For example: I'm Frank's daughter and Maryanne's best friend; I live in a Connecticut suburb; I love chocolate, the color purple, and yellow Labrador retrievers; I'm a lifelong liberal and member of the Catholic Church; I'm a successful doctor who owns a large condo; I'm a serious substance abuser; I belong to a country club and a good social set; I'm an A-list person. We all think this way.

Buddhism regularly reminds us that all of these things— people, objects, ideas, accomplishments, habits, addictions, memories, and even opinions—represent our attachments. These attachments are what connect us to life on this planet. Buddhists are not alone in this philosophy. My first guru was a saintly Hindu sage named Neem Karoli Baba, a wandering holy man of great age. When he died in 1973, he was called a jivamukta, a liberated spiritual soul. Neem Karoli Baba taught, "Don't get attached to wealth, people, and pets. Better to cleave to God and truth." Neem Karoli Baba devoted his life to finding liberation from the ties that bind us to the earthly plane.

Our overweening attachments are said to be the cause of our suffering. Because we are focused on our attachments, we fail to pay attention to the truth of the present moment; we fail to follow our deeper values. If we insist on desiring those things that are fleeting, we set ourselves up for disappointment and dissatisfaction; when we insist on clinging to those things that are unreliable, we become candidates for unhappiness. If we cling to unreality, we lose our sanity.

Attachment is all about wanting and not wanting. It's about desire and dislike. Attachment, clinging, craving, greed, lust, and desire on the one hand, and aversion, aggression, anger, hatred, enmity, and dislike, on the other. What do you want most in your life? What do you want least? What attracts you? What repels you? We don't all like the same things; we don't all dislike the same things. These are mere personal preferences. Nonetheless, we all know how intensely we can want and not want something—and it can be pretty much anything. The Buddha taught that neither pleasure nor pain are ultimately very satisfying; both are fleeting. No matter how much we have or don't have, we keep seeking satisfaction and fulfillment. We fail to experience contentment.

Buddhist cosmology talks about three different realms of existence: desire, form, and formlessness. The realm that we humans all inhabit is known as the Realm of Desire. Here in the Realm of Desire we are motivated by urges and reactions based mainly on what we like and don't like. We become attached to people and things we find desirable or attractive. When we want something, whether it be to spend the afternoon with that special someone or to buy the biggest house in town, we try to draw the object of our desire closer; we want it to be part of our personal experience. When we are driven and motivated by our habitual likes and dislikes, we are tossed about by karmic winds that blow us uncontrollably in all sorts of directions without leaving us much chance to choose or navigate.

Not that long ago, a friend visited a nursery school and saw a paper hanging on a wall. On it was something humorously entitled "The Toddler's Creed." She copied it down.

The Toddler's Creed

If I want it, it's mine.
If I give it to you and then change my mind, it's mine.
If I can take it away from you by force, it's mine.
If I had it a little while ago, it's mine.
If we are playing with something together, then all the
    pieces are mine.
If it looks just like the one I used to own or have at home,
    it's mine.

When it comes to attachments, in many ways we are all still two-year-old toddlers. "Mine" translates into "me, myself, and I" pretty soon in human development. This self-centered attitude is the root of evil and unhappiness, for who really possesses our body and our possessions, and for how long? Walking the spiritual path to enlightenment implies that we are trying to be a little less toddler-like regarding our attachments.

Probably the easiest attachments to examine are those that are primarily superficial. We all have many superficial attachments, don't we? We're attached to our food, our jewelry, our furniture, and our clothing; we're attached to our musical instruments, our CD collections, and our sports equipment; we're attached to our computers, our faxes, and our comfortable office chairs. We're attached to our houses, apartments, neighborhoods, cars, art collections, and TV sets. Don't forget our TV sets. And how about the fancy DVD players. We also become dependent and attached in other ways. Personally, I have no preference in terms of dry cleaning, but my wife Kathy says that she is very attached to her dry cleaning establishment and will never take her clothes anywhere else.

Then there are the deeper levels of attachment that we naturally form with the people in our lives. We are attached to our families and loved ones; we are attached to our mates, our children, our lovers, our friends, and, of course, our precious animal companions. These are the beings we love and who love us. How could we not feel attached to them? In some instances we feel attached at the hip; when life separates us from our loved ones, the pain associated with the physical wrench can be overwhelming. These all-too-human attachments are the most complicated. They are the most rewarding, as well as the ones most fraught with irritations and challenges.

When the Buddha began his path to enlightenment, not only did he walk away from his attachment to wealth and comfort, he also walked away from his attachment to his young wife, infant son, and the rest of his family and friends. Monks who go forth alone regularly loosen the ties of attachment to friends and family, but most of us aren't entirely ready to renounce earthly love, family, and home.

Monks such as the Dalai Lama, Thich Nhat Hanh, and my own Buddhist gurus and teachers have shown me that celibacy and letting go of attachment to sexuality is a beautiful way of life, although it is certainly not for everyone. I myself experienced it for half a dozen years during cloistered meditation retreat in the eighties, as well as during several year-long stays in Tibetan monasteries in the Himalayas in the seventies. Monks and nuns vow to refrain from sexual activities in order to simplify their lives and loosen the grip of desire. They sublimate their sexual passion and energy, refocusing that natural drive and turning it toward a higher, deeper, more deathless object or goal. In this way they train in devoting themselves entirely to spiritual practice. I found that refraining from intimate relationships did not keep me from forming loving, quite interesting, platonic friendships with women, including both nuns and laywomen. There are so many ways to share closeness in this life, including spiritual, cling-free relationships.

Having strong internal boundaries as well as external behavioral vows helped focus and refine my energy. It developed both my sense of equanimity and feelings of inner detachment; it also deepened the intensity of my spiritual fervor—all so useful in the inner quest, which is often like spiritual mountaineering: The less you carry, the easier the climb. I found the practice of nonclinging to particular persons over and above others helped me develop and experience a more hospitable, welcoming, accepting, and open heart. It freed me from the petty jealousies, desires, elation, and disappointment of the usual hurly-burly of emotional relations that I had experienced in ordinary single life during my youthful years. Chaste living balanced with appropriate spiritual practices in the framework of a supportive community helped me learn to see beyond my attachments. It taught me how to love those I don't particularly like. This was a major learning.

Many of us have been conditioned to believe that another person is going to "save me." Be honest now, don't we all want to believe the following myth? "All I have to do is find the Prince (or Princess) Charming of my dreams, who will complete and satisfy me in every way, then my life will be perfect." Recognizing the emptiness of this illusion and living in solitude opens up space for the inner face of divinity to emerge within one's own heart-mind. Then one begins to find God and the beloved everywhere in everything, always. Life becomes your lover. This is the secret of celibacy as an authentically meaningful spiritual practice. Those on the spiritual path choose celibacy not because there is anything intrinsically wrong with healthy sexuality, but because there is a lot more to life than a preoccupation with that. I found that good monastic training in the Buddhist tradition can help interested seekers develop in this profoundly spiritual way.

Buddhism teaches that refraining from forming intense attachments lessens the suffering that inevitably follows the change, losses, and disappointments of life. For some of us, the idea of living without close personal relationships may seem harsh. This is a choice that each of us has to make individually. I have found no one more buoyant and spirited than my Buddhist teachers, although many of them did not partake of the joys of sex, parenting, and family life. The cultivation of nonattachment includes the development of a genuine certainty and conviction about reality and where long-lasting satisfaction and fulfillment truly lie. Mere sensual pleasure cannot satisfy anyone for long. That is why Yoga and Tantric traditions teach us not to condemn or shun the world, but to sacrilize it by treating the body and the world itself like a temple and all beings like gods and goddesses. Then we can find within our own experience of life that we carry a portable paradise within the heart.

Inner detachment, remember, is not synonymous with indifference. We do still care about others, as well as social justice issues and concerns, but we are far less invested in desirable outcomes. Inner balance and equanimity help us feel clearer and less volatile about what we are doing and why. We can flow better and roll more gracefully with the rollicking punches and weaving bumpy roadways of life.

Inner detachment leaves room for a welling up of other heart virtues, including caring, compassion, and a loving-kindness that is more inclusive and less partial and self-referential; it opens us to the real possibility of seeing all beings as members of our extended family. Developed nonattachment helps protect us from the worst feelings of grievous loss we experience when we lose loved ones. Although, of course, even monks and nuns have homelands, parents, siblings, close friends, pets, and spiritual brethren that they inevitably lose and grieve over at some time in their lives. Tibet's solitary wanderer Patrul Rinpoche said, "One pound of possessions and attachments is like one pound of burden to cast aside." Mark Twain said, "If a man could have half his wishes, he could double his troubles."

Having an overweening attachment to one's sports car, condo, or VCR is very different from being attached to one's family. We have all been taught that we get our greatest satisfaction from the love of family, and for most of us that is probably true. It's difficult living without this dimension of human love. But even if one has found a perfect soul mate, blissful as that union may be, it will one day come to an end. Ultimately, even the pleasure one takes from a satisfying family life is fleeting and impermanent. In the end, all dependable satisfaction comes from the higher ground above and within, depending on how we choose to look at it. True satisfaction comes from the deathless dimension, not the temporary, transient, ephemeral, and material realm of joining and parting; it comes from a more invisible dimension, not merely from our plans and stratagem. Thus we rely on the ubiquitous religious impulse in human beings to find a love that transcends death—a life that goes beyond this world where, as they say, moth and rust can destroy and corrupt. There is no way around this. This is not to denigrate our quotidian ordinary concerns, rather it is a way to bring deeper perspective to daily life, a way to bring a sense of the eternal into this time and space and in that way get perspective on our existence. We bring the timeless dimension right into the here and now. This is the realm of faith, of invisible connections, of interrelatedness.

Let's look at some of our other attachments. We are attached to good health. When we are young, most of us take it completely for granted. We are attached to our bodies—our arms, legs, abundant hair, and unlined skin; we are attached to youth, beauty, and physical strength. When our bodies begin to fail us, it fills us with fear and sometimes anger. Age is something that happens to other people—older people. "Not to me, not to me!" the inner toddler wails.

There are yet other forms of attachment that we all make. We become attached to our opinions and theories. We become attached to the stories we tell ourselves about who we are and what we think. We become inordinately attached to our status, accomplishments, and reputations—and what we think they say about us. We become attached to our biases, and habitual way of doing things. We become attached to religion and political preference; we even become attached to our fears and anxieties. "Who would I be if I gave up my problems?" the inner adolescent asks. There are people in our culture, like Woody Allen, who have built their creative careers around the glorification of their neurotic, and often amusing, attitudes.

Why is it so hard to let go of even superficial attachments? Impossible even? The fact is that most of us have a love-hate relationship with change. We like change, and we don't like change. We like new and different things, and yet we are attached to the familiar. Comfort food and comforting habits are examples of the ways we cling to familiar routines and ruts. Often we cling to habits that aren't even comforting or satisfying simply because we are unable to let go or explore new ways to do things. Think of all the people who hang on to their addictions or stay in abusive relationships because they are resistant to change. Individual change and transformation can be difficult. It takes guts. And sometimes it requires outside help.

Yet, it is also true that this society devotedly worships at the "shrine of the new." New gadgets, new clothes, not to mention new friends, seem so fascinating and exciting. We even feel a little younger as we set foot into a new car or new relationship, don't we? The new technology is so overwhelming that many of us can't begin to understand it, even as we purchase the new computer we "must" have for our work. We are understandably ambivalent. I personally am still stymied by the VCR in our living room. I think about the old VCR with which I was just beginning to establish a relationship. Why did it have to break? Why was this change necessary? Why did I have to lose this attachment—my old friend that I could program and manage? I am reminded of my grandmother clinging to her old rotary phone in the digital age.

Things seem to be changing faster here in the twenty-first century than ever before. Technological advances have certainly been more exponential than incremental. Our computers are obsolete almost before they are out of the packing box. No sense in becoming attached to that old operating system, although I know people who are still bemoaning the loss of older versions of computer programs with which they were cozily familiar. Politicians soar to the top of the polls one day only to sink to the bottom the next. And what about relationships? Some people seem to have become experts at forming superficial attachments that they can easily break. Multiple marriages are the norm, not the exception.

One of my favorite poets is Emily Dickinson, who was born in Massachusetts in 1830. She had her heart torn asunder as a young woman and spent the rest of her life trying to recover from that attachment. Today, I know people who claim that their hearts are broken a half dozen times a year. Does that mean that lovers today are less attached than those of yesteryear? Does it mean that lovers today are more fickle than those in the nineteenth century? Or does it mean that we are less attached to what our neighbors and family might think of us if we speedily transition from relationship to relationship?

Consider all the intense ups and downs that everyone goes through. We feel joy; we feel depressed; we feel sad; we feel elated; we feel crushed; we feel disappointment; we feel resentment. We live with the fear of terrorism and the grief associated with profound loss; we abide with the sadness connected to lost opportunities. Don't we all know both the joys of companionship and the pangs of loneliness? How about the feelings associated with financial gain and loss? We get a good return on real estate investments, and we feel elated; the stock market goes up, and we congratulate ourselves on our savvy stock picks; it crashes, and we feel crushed. So many different feelings emerge in a single week, day, or even hour. That's what it means to be living and breathing. Being overly invested in our momentary triumphs leaves us vulnerable to disappointment. Expecting good things to last and unwanted things to stay away forever is simply unrealistic, even when we are amid good karma and bounty aplenty.

The goal of Buddhism is to help seekers realize the facts of change and impermanence and get beyond attachment to the momentary ups and downs of this world. In this way we find something permanent and reliable in which to take refuge and experience inner peace. This is called Nirvana, everlasting bliss.

EXAMINING OUR GREATEST ATTACHMENTS

When any of our attachments—whether they be to people, places, things, opinions, beliefs, or ideas—change, we change the way we define ourselves and thus we change accordingly. If we want to create change in our lives, we simply have to change some of the things we are attached to.

There are many things that all of us are attached to, but the question is, just how attached are we to them? How much do we identify with them and feel we can't do without them? How invested are we in those things that seem so important to us? Can we live without them?

Let me remind you again that nonattachment is not complacency. It doesn't imply a lack of caring and commitment. The philosophy of nonattachment is based in the understanding that holding on too tightly to those things, which in any case are always going to be slipping through our fingers, hurts and gives us rope burn. This is the secret of letting go. Holding on with a control-freak type of grip—as if any of us are really totally in charge—simply keeps us stuck and costs us our freedom. Therefore it is in our higher self-interest to let go a little, as appropriate, and enjoy things as they come and go without overly investing in their permanence or lasting reality.

Seekers work on developing a greater sense of nonattachment

and cultivating inner detachment; seekers are striving to have a larger, nonworldly, longer-range, transpersonal, unselfish perspective. I know I am. Yet I know how difficult it is to let go of attachments; this doesn't happen overnight. Like many people, for example, I find it difficult to let go of my attachment to outcomes. When I was a kid and playing sports every day I learned that it was better to enjoy the game without being overly invested in the result. It was more fun that way, and far more sane and friendly too. In theory and in practice, I know that there is greater satisfaction and peace of mind to be found simply by doing the best one can and then letting go of the results. T. S. Eliot said, "For us there is only the trying. The rest is not our business." Nonetheless, like most people, if I manage to resist the temptation of eating that large piece of chocolate cake, I want to know that I am going to lose weight. I want that desired outcome, and I am disappointed when I don't get it. I continue to work at letting go of my attachment to outcomes—and it does take time.

Ask yourself:

What are my greatest attachments? What are the things that I think I can't live without? Is it status? Security? A nice place to live? Good food? Satisfying work? Sex?

In your head, let go of one of these attachments and see how it feels. Imagine yourself living a different life than the one you now enjoy, perhaps without the apartment and job you are attached to. Let it drop away. How does it feel? Do you feel lighter? Or do anxieties arise?

Experiment in your head with letting go of things you think are important. Let go of one attachment at a time. How would your life change? What would happen, for example, if you gave up the apartment or house you live in and moved into someplace smaller or less expensive? Would you need less money to live on and would that make you feel less driven and encumbered? How about most of your clothes and gear?

What are the ideas and beliefs to which you are most attached?

What can you let go or change? What would happen if you let go of your particular worldview, for example? How would you perceive things differently? What about your attachment to a group or a preferred political party or religion? How would you be different if you let go of these attachments? How would you be changed without these beliefs? What would be missing? Who would you be without those external roles, identities, and place-markers?

What are the stories about yourself to which you are most attached? Are you really who you think you are? Do you tend to see yourself in a certain way? Are you inclined to view yourself as unique and special, or as the underdog? Perhaps even the victim? Do you look for ways that you can affirm your version of yourself? Do you live your life in such a way that your story of what happens between you and others will always be the same? Do you see yourself as the caretaker or "giver" in any relationship? Do you see yourself as the smartest person in the room? The least informed? The most out to lunch? Are you the shyest? The most neurotic? The least privileged? The most overworked? These exaggerations all represent clinging to fixed ideas and self-images.

How are you attached to these stories you tell yourself? What would happen to your life if you changed them?

How about the people in your life? Is it really true that you can't live without him or her? For just a few minutes, how would it feel to entertain the opposite thought? This is scary, but try it out just for experimental purposes. Say, "I don't need him/her." "I can live without him/her." How does it feel? Try to actually feel and experience that, just for a moment. No outer action is required.

How attached are you to transcendent qualities and virtues such as peace and harmony, mental and spiritual health, wholeness and well-being, equality and justice, the greater good of the planet? Can you see the ways that these values are reflected or denied in the attachments you have formed to people, things, or ideas?

A Little Tibetan Practice Advice on Letting Go of Who You Used to Be

Once my old teacher told me, as a meditation instruction, to use visualization, clothes, props, behavior, words, or whatever comes to mind to pretend to be anyone besides who you think you are. Try that out, try it on, see how it feels, and see that shifting is possible, however momentarily, from out of our habitually held identity and self-image and all that comes with it.

> *All things found in the world and beyond*
> *Are illusions created by one's own concepts.*
> *Grasping at them but further distorts perception.*
> *Give up grasping and see things as they are.*

THE SEVENTH DALAI LAMA

CHAPTER FIVE

Letting Go of

Holding On

Don't be afraid. Just play the music.

CHARLIE PARKER

Anyone who has ever seen the movie *Citizen Kane* remembers the mystery surrounding the name "Rosebud." It is the last word uttered by Kane, the central character, who dies a lonely man in a huge house surrounded by the many expensive possessions that he has accumulated throughout his lifetime. Why is this aged tycoon calling out for Rosebud? The viewer wonders who or what it represents. Finally we get to the scene that shows a child's simple wooden sled burning in an old furnace; a close-up reveals the word "Rosebud" printed on the sled. Oh, we think, Rosebud was his sled when he was a little boy. Why did Charles Foster Kane hold on to this old childhood sled? Why did he hold on to this memory, this word? Why didn't he ever let it go?

I think about some of the things I hold on to: I have my father's address book, his GI card from the army, as well as his 1945 discharge papers. I have my grandfather's passport and driver's license. Among my other keepsakes are also my grandfather's tallis and tefillin, my father's old prayer book, his tallis, tefillin, and yarmulke, as well as my own tallis, yarmulke, and the prayer-book from my own Bar Mitzvah ceremony, which took place in January 1964 at Temple Gates of Zion in Valley Stream, New York. I keep them all together in a drawer in my night table. A stranger going through my possessions might assume that I am praying in a synagogue most Saturdays instead of meditating on retreat. Or that I use these holy things more than I do. I also still have my very worn out Rawlings baseball glove from my halcyon days at first base and on the pitcher's mound in junior high and high school. My boyhood name, Jeff Miller, is still inscribed on the strap along with a Long Island phone number. The glove represents who I used to be during that period of my life.

Some of us have been left with the task of cleaning out the houses and apartments of relatives or friends who have recently died. We go through their belongings, and we wonder why they kept certain things. I have a friend who cleaned out her father's bedroom after his death; in a drawer she discovered more than sixty pipes, a box of expensive cigars, a couple dozen cigarette lighters, and a half dozen cigarette cases. To the best of her knowledge, her father had never smoked. What was he thinking? Why was he holding on to these things? She herself kept one of the cigars, still wrapped in aging cellophane. She holds on to the memory of her father's inexplicable collection and to him in this harmless little way.

Of course, as a philosophical concept, *holding on* goes much deeper than merely retaining articles of sentimental value. There are so many complex levels of holding on. We all engage in them. Don't we all know people who are so totally stuck in a groove that it is obvious to everyone around them that they are holding on to patterns that no longer have any use? We joke about their knee-jerk reactions, predictable thinking, and equally predictable behavior. Sometimes we see it in exterior things—Great Aunt Sally, for example, who is still wearing the pageboy hair style she first adopted sixty years ago, or Cousin Lennie, a perennial bachelor who has been searching for Ms. Right for the last forty years.

We all hold on to habits that are difficult to explain, but some of us are more oriented to habit than others. When my father commuted by car from Long Island to work in New York City every day, he would get up early to listen to the traffic report before he started out. After retiring from his accounting job, he continued to do the same thing. For some reason, hearing what was happening on the 59th Street Bridge, the Long Island Expressway, and the Queens Midtown Tunnel on weekday mornings continued to bring him a sense of comfort and familiarity. It held importance equal to the morning news and national report. Holding on to comfort and familiarity often makes great sense. The eighteenth-century German philosopher Immanuel Kant was so routinized and predictable in his habits that the people of his town used the time by which he left on his daily walk to set their clocks.

Holding on to a habit like a daily walk seems pretty harmless and even admirable. But think about the intensity with which we dogmatically hold on to our opinions and beliefs. Don't we often do damage to ourselves and others by determinedly clutching at opinions and beliefs that have little or no objective reality? Think about married couples fighting over the right temperature at which to set the thermostat or the correct way to stack the dishwasher. They each have strong opinions and arguments for a specific point of view. Watching sitcom couples struggle with this level of unresolved conflict can occasionally be funny. Living this way can be painful.

The Buddha taught that it is usually a mistake to believe that any opinion or situation is objectively good or bad since everything depends on the perspective of the viewer. We see this in the horror of war, where one side can be rejoicing over the body count while the other is mourning its losses. Each side is attached to and invested in its own beliefs and opinions and holding on, no matter what the cost. What we each have in our lives thus are wanted and unwanted experiences, which are almost entirely dependent on individual opinions, preferences, and desires.

We suffer because of a lack of validly knowing and understanding reality, what it is and how it works. The Buddha taught that it is like a group of blind men touching an elephant and then trying to describe what an elephant is. The one holding a leg says that an elephant is like a pillar, the one holding the tail emphatically says that it is like a rope, while the one confronting its side is quite sure the elephant is a wall. Because we are not totally aware or conscious, we have little ability to see and comprehend the whole.

I don't often listen to talk radio, but when by chance I do, I find myself being shocked by the amount of energy that some of the radio hosts and callers-in expend defending the positions that they hold on to with all their might. I've heard commentators arguing their particular political opinions with a zeal that is hard to comprehend. Why do they hold on so tightly? What is really at stake? Why do defenders of the death penalty, for example, insist on the wisdom of their position even when it has been shown that the death penalty is no deterrent to crime, the system is imperfect, and that a significantly large percentage of innocent men and women have been put to death? I raise the issue of the death penalty because I know it is one of particular concern to the Dalai Lama. (He is against capital punishment, by the way, and so am I.) But we all have opinions on the death penalty, and we cling to them, don't we?

Buddhists often use the word *clinging* as a synonym for holding on. Sometimes "clinging" or "holding on" to an opinion, idea, or training works in a positive way. Doctors hold on to and retain much of the education and information they received, and we all experience the benefit when they share what they know. Charismatic talk-show hosts expound on their cherished opinions, and they make an enviable living, which works out for them and their families. When we get in our cars, holding on to the wheel makes it more likely that we will be returning home in the evening. There are ways in which we all need to hold on. Otherwise we wouldn't be able to live and function on this planet. There are many degrees of holding on: daily routines, dogmatic beliefs and prejudices, psychological fixations, phobias, and addictions, are all varieties of holding on. The issue is the extent to which holding on limits our freedom to vary from habitual patterns and conditioning. Questioning and examining our individual patterns are part of the Buddha's recipe for awakening from the sleep of illusion and delusion. The Third Zen Patriarch said long ago, "Do not seek for truth; merely cease to cherish opinions."

Mindlessly and rigidly holding on to anything exacts a heavy price. Think about how much energy and attention we have invested in maintaining and holding together our own self-image and persona. What a relief it is when we let down our guard and allow ourselves to be authentic and real. When we stop holding on, it's a little like taking off our shoes and allowing ourselves to relax. It's like taking a breather in the midst of hard work. It feels very good.

The self is not a solid entity, yet we congeal around that self-concept until it becomes a continuous activity centered around a tightly held, cherished egotism. From this, all kinds of mischievous forms of selfishness arise. Buddhists say that we suffer as a result of clinging to the belief in a self; we suffer as a result of our believing that things are permanent; we suffer because we believe that things truly, objectively, lastingly exist. We suffer because we think that our opinions and concerns are important and have lasting reality.

We take ourselves so seriously that we tend to believe that our moods and emotions are real entities. When Andy, for example, gets angry with his twin sister Rachel, his feelings are so intense that, for the moment at least, he wants to annihilate her. Fortunately for Rachel, Andy's method of attack is limited to sarcasm and withering looks. Usually Andy's anger blows over within a short period of time. In fact, as soon as Andy sees tears well up in Rachel's eyes, his anger turns to sadness and guilt. He realizes he has been mean, and he tries to make it up to her. For her part, Rachel says she understands, although she actually doesn't, and she usually has some form of passive-aggressive feedback that will quickly reignite Andy's fury. Andy and Rachel have been playing out versions of this scenario since the days when they shared a playpen. Why don't they ever let it go and develop more evolved and mature ways of working things through? The bigger question, of course, is: Why can't any of us ever let go of our need to "win," or "be right," or just "show up the other guy"? Too often we would rather be right than happy and in harmony. The cost of this kind of clinging can be immense.

LET IT GO

Maria is still crying over a husband who walked out on her and their infant daughter over a year ago. "Let it go!" her best friend advises. "He isn't worth it. Get on with your life."

Richard feels that his boss humiliates him and is purposely setting him up for failure. He feels tremendous anger and resentment and carries this attitude with him to work every day. His coworkers tell him that their boss is just crazy and treats everybody the same way. "Let it go!" they tell him. "Don't take it personally."

Mike feels that his mother and father lacked basic parenting skills and left him ill prepared for life. He still feels hurt and angry over their treatment. On family holidays when they come to visit, all he wants to do is sit in a corner and seethe. "Let it go!" his wife pleads. "That was then; this is now."

Monica is trying to overcome years of addictive and codependent behavior. She knows how vulnerable she is and how easy it is for her to fall back into old, worn-out patterns. "Let go and let God!" her support group chants. This often helps her to do just that.

Trixie and Dixie are two cute little cairn terriers who share a home and an intense rivalry. They compete over everything, including their owner's attention. Whenever one picks up a dog toy, the other automatically wants it. "Can't you let anything go?" their owner wails as she intervenes between two yelping dogs.

Recently I was at a retreat center in Switzerland. One of the office workers, Eva, had a little yellow sticker on her computer, right above her mouse pad. It said, "Let Go or Get Dragged." I find myself remembering that little mouse and smiling every time I do. That is one wise woman.

"Letting go" has become a buzzword among Buddhists, yoga students, and New Agers. But what exactly does it mean? And how do we do it? How do we stop clinging? How do we let go of our compulsions and fixations? And what is the difference between letting go and merely throwing things away? The secret is this: Letting go means letting things come and go by just *letting be.*

Rather than thinking of liberation at some future time, it can be found through the practice of letting go of little things, one at a time, here and now. Letting go means learning to lighten up as well as enlightening up. We do this by loosening our tight grip on things and relaxing our tendency to try to control everything in our environment. If we are unable to do this, we run the risk of being pulled along, or "dragged," willy-nilly without conscious awareness. We end up where we would not choose to be. Unfortunately, too many of us are paying members of the worldwide church of control-freakism. And the dues can become outrageous.

The first step in letting go is self-awareness. How can we begin to practice letting go and letting be when we don't clearly see what we are doing? We need to become conscious of any tendency we have to be close-fisted and grasping. We need to become aware of all the ways in which we cling to old behaviors and moods. We need to become aware of our vested interest in tired opinions and attitudes; we need to see all the ways in which we are narrow-minded or dogmatic. Of course, all of this is easier said than done.

Do any of us really see all the ways in which we are clinging and holding on to objects, people, feelings, ideas, and beliefs which serve no real value in our lives? Think of the toddler refusing to let go of a toy; think of the crying child who is insistent about hanging on to his belief that something dangerous is lurking beneath his bed; think of the puppy who won't let go of whatever little treasure he's got in his mouth. Think of the tiger with meat in his teeth; sometimes we are equally tenacious beyond rhyme or reason.

A couple of weeks ago I was on a supermarket express line. The customer in front of me became convinced that another shopper was trying to get into line with too many items. She became enraged, her reaction blown far out of proportion, and yet she couldn't let it go. "That's what I hate about people," she exclaimed vociferously to anyone who cared to listen. "Doesn't anybody care about rules anymore? Can't anybody count? Everybody is so damned inconsiderate!" Maybe she had just had a bad day, but at that moment, she was so angry that the sight of a supermarket customer in the express lane with one extra can of tuna fish put her over the top. She couldn't let it go. How does that benefit anyone?

The practice of letting go asks a lot of us. On an external level, think about all the things that we don't want to relinquish. Think about possessions, money, youth, people, accomplishments, career, and status. On an internal level, notice how we cling to self-concepts and images, to our ideas, opinions, beliefs, politics, and habitual ways of doing things; think about how attached we are to our feelings, moods, regrets, grudges, memories, and the stories we tell ourselves. Think about all the ways we try to hold on to and control all the aspects of our lives.

On the innermost level, reflect on how we don't want to let go of our egoistic, selfish, self-important view of self and who we think we are. As we walk the spiritual path to enlightenment, ego-clinging is what we are really attempting to shed. We want to let go of and empty out our separatist tendencies and our selfish agendas. Letting go on this level takes time and practice; it also takes self-knowledge and awareness. Letting go of ego is the real test of our spiritual evolvement. There is no external renunciation or sacrifice that can match selflessness. Nonattachment is the supreme spiritual discipline; nonclinging is the ultimate form of generosity; unconditional love is the greatest spiritual virtue.

Letting go of egoism is tough spiritual work. It's so easy to get caught up in the emotional highs that occur when our ego is being stroked. I have a friend, a fine artist, who always says that she wishes she didn't have to attend her own shows and exhibits. She finds that they are troubling arenas for the ego, and this is true whether she is feeling successful or insecure. Either way, her ego can too easily take hold; she prefers to stay centered and concentrate on her work as she is doing it. She says that she tries to practice a kind of Zen removal from her work once it is finished, and doesn't want to think about whether it sells or is even well reviewed because that has little to do with the practice of making art.

Spiritual teachers and leaders also have to wrestle with the angels of egotism as well as the demons of illusions and negative emotion. When I first left the Tibetan Buddhist monastery in which I had lived for eight years, I was pushing forty. I had no appointments and no disappointments. I had few material possessions to relinquish because I had no property, no car, no computer, no credit cards, no health plan, and nobody was in any way dependent on me. I had no financial worries because there were no finances to speak of. I only started to have financial issues in my mid-forties when I started to have income and assets. I was a living example of the teaching that possessions are like baggage and only weigh you down. When we start accumulating things, we can easily get out of balance. Instead of having just enough ballast to keep our little personal ships upright, we end up having so much in the cargo hold that our ship can hardly maneuver on the seas of life, even if it doesn't quite sink.

After leaving the monastery, I began teaching and writing, living as a Dharma teacher without a fixed abode. Then in my mid-forties, I had some worldly success, which I've certainly enjoyed and been grateful for. However, I've had to laugh at myself and realize that with this success came ambition, which of course is directly connected to the ego. What is ambition, after all, but an attempt to feed and enlarge the ego—to shore up the small self that is always lurking? That is why Tibetan tradition teaches that worldly success can be an obstacle on the path of enlightenment.

I have to remember to keep my ego from becoming overly attached or invested in the business of publishing books, for example. Instead of simply writing books, and then letting them go out into the world to make their own way, like grown children, I sometimes find that I become overly attached to the book's success or failure. I have to watch myself closely to avoid worrying about how well the books are selling, whether or not the publisher is doing a good job, and if the reviewers write appreciative words. Thinking about these things too much can make me feel frustrated and unhappy. I've learned that the less I think of my own progress or success, the better my mood and the more content I feel.

The Peace Master Shantideva said, "Happiness in this world comes from thinking less about ourselves and more about the well-being of others. Unhappiness comes from being preoccupied with the self." I don't know about other teachers, but I know I have to watch myself and not take myself too seriously; I always try to continue doing my own spiritual practice. Day to day I remain a student of Buddhism. This makes me happy and keeps me grounded.

When I first started teaching in 1990 I asked one of my favorite young incarnate lamas, Drukchen Rinpoche, for some advice. He said, "Remember why you are here, and remember why they are there." What he meant was that students come because they are looking for something to guide and help them. I am in the role of teacher because I was fortunate enough to have been exposed to the Dharma and to have trained with so many of the great guardians of the spiritual legacy and treasure of Tibetan Buddhism. The wise lama was telling me to remember that this wasn't all about me and to be careful not to become complacent and self-satisfied. Another master said, "Don't become too comfortable." Our own American teacher, Harinam

Das, helps me stay straight with Zen utterances such as, "There is nothing to teach, no one to teach it, and nobody to listen."

LETTING GO OF KARMIC BAGGAGE

On some level we all repeat self-destructive patterns in our lives, don't we? Why does Susan keep entering into relationships with unfaithful partners, for example? Yes, of course, we can fault her partners for being dishonest and unfair. But if Susan is really interested in taking a deeper look at her situation, she has to acknowledge that she is a party to these relationships. What is she holding on to that allows her to be in these relationships? Could it be a view of herself as victim? Could it be old feelings of unworthiness and unskillful patterns of relating that she learned from her parents? Why does she always handle her relationships the same way? Why does she hold on so tightly to her fears of being alone that she will tolerate almost anything? It looks as though she is clinging to that old saw, "beggars can't be choosers." Why does she fall into such an unfortunate way of thinking?

Men and women with codependency issues can be heavily burdened: Sometimes they don't know how to let go of their tendency to overprotect loved ones; sometimes they fall back on failed coping skills like nagging, arguing, self-abnegation, or attempts to manipulate. They need to know that letting go in relationships isn't synonymous with loving less. Internal detachment and objectivity can help us love with fewer conditions and more generosity of spirit.

We all have areas in our own lives where much of our karmic baggage is buried. Few of us, for example, know how to let go of old hurts and relationships. I know a man whose wife left him for another person about two years ago. He hasn't been able to let any of it go. He acknowledges that the marriage was seriously flawed, but he can't release his anger or his feeling of having been betrayed and humiliated. This tortures him daily, almost as if someone is doing it to him again and again. Letting go of failed relationships and lost love are among the most difficult things that any of us have to cope with in life. We hate to see our shiny dreams dashed. It hurts. Many feel nostalgic for "the good old days," even when the nostalgia is completely illusory, based mostly on selective memory and fantasy about the past.

The lesson of "letting go" appears and reappears in everyone's life in myriad ways. Recently I spoke to a woman I know named Phyllis. She told me that she was having problems getting along with her grown son and was beginning to see that her primary problem in the relationship was that she was unable to acknowledge that he was an adult who was capable of taking care of himself. She couldn't let go of the role she used to play when he was still a little child. Her son didn't help matters any, because he also too easily fell into a childlike, dependent role with her. He told her all his problems with his girlfriend and his job. She responded by trying to fix things, as she would have done when he was a little boy. He then reacted by becoming angry and accusing her of interfering. Phyllis and her son love each other, but they are stuck. Phyllis is struggling to learn to let go of her need to control and her need to have her opinion heard. Phyllis says that when her son asked for advice, she used to give it. Then she would call the next day to talk about it some more and to see if he followed it. Now, she simply speaks her mind, and she wills herself to let the entire conversation go. "I've had to learn that whatever my son does is his own business," she told me. "I've had to let go, and it feels a lot better!"

If we are trying to get a sense of where our karmic baggage is stored, I think it helps to look at those places where we have the hardest time letting go. Some people have a difficult time letting go of money or their youthful good looks; others prefer to cling to a self-aggrandizing belief that they are always right or are somehow unique or special. Different people can't let go of various feelings like jealousy, pride, bitterness, resentment, envy, or even fear. Some carry deep grudges that eat at the innards like a form of emotional cancer.

For all of us, much of the sadness in life can be traced to our problems with letting go. The Buddhist Heart Sutra reminds us that ultimately everything is going, going, gone, gone, beyond and away. Swaha! Gone-zo! So be it. Okay.

LETTING GO AND PICKING UP

The concepts of letting go and nonattachment are part and parcel of all the great religious traditions. Christians around the world, for example, give something up for a period in the church calendar known as Lent. They choose to "let go" of something they desire in their lives, knowing that this relinquishment leaves room for something else to arrive or enter. Some people let go of negative habits such as smoking for Lent; some people let go of their need for a special food or treat like ice cream. In the Islamic tradition, Muslims regularly fast each year during the month of Ramadan; they give up eating and drinking during the daylight hours. When done in a spiritual or religious context, letting go is more than a random act. It's called renunciation and it implies a letting go of earthly satisfaction in return for a closer connection and alliance with the divine. Sometimes we must lighten our load in the pursuit of spiritual fulfillment. My own experience is that finding the divine in our lives is usually more a matter of subtraction than addition.

When monks and nuns turn away from a worldly life, more is involved than merely renouncing and letting go of old baggage, peripheral worldly preoccupations, and habitual concerns. They are also taking up a new way of life that brings them closer to the center of their being; they are letting go of worldly desires in order to be closer to their spiritual center. They are not just walking or turning away; they are also turning toward something deeper and more meaningful.

This is an important thing to remember about the act of relinquishment and letting go. As spiritual seekers we are trying to let go of the negative and pick up and move forward with something that is more positive, wholesome, and beneficial. We let go of destructive habits and assume a healthier lifestyle, for example. We let go of greed and practice generosity. We let go of anger in favor of love, tolerance, and compassion; we let go of jealousy in favor of peace and rejoicing in the good fortunes of others; we let go of judgmental attitudes in favor of more accepting and open-minded points of view. We let go of overly controlling behavior by learning to relax our tight grip on reality and meeting life on its own terms, taking it as it comes. It's not so hard to evolve consciously in this way through the active practice of letting go. Open hands, open arms, open heart, open eyes, open mind. This helps further faith, trust, and a deepening conviction. It is extraordinarily wise to do so.

MEDITATION AS A TRAINING FOR LETTING GO

Westerners are drawn to Buddhism for a wide variety of reasons, but many are specifically attracted because they want to learn to let go of afflicted states of mind that are making them unhappy. Some want to let go of anxieties. Some want to let go of fears. Some want to let go of obsessive thoughts. Students will often approach me saying things like, "I want to let go of my codependency; I want to let go of my angry feelings toward my mother, but it is so hard!" Others say they can't relax and meditate because they think far too much, often letting old and painful thoughts take over. Letting go and achieving detachment requires some level of self-mastery. It always requires the cultivation of self-awareness and a healthy discipline.

Remember that taking the spiritual path always includes traveling inward to learn as much as we can about ourselves. Think about the term "traveling inward." Reflect on what that means. Our nightly dreams attest to the fact that the inner landscape is a rich, phantasmagorical world filled with our private demons as well as our own heavenly helpers. In Buddhism that inner landscape is called "mind." In fact, Buddhism is known as a "science of the mind," as much as a religion. It is seen as a way of refining and cultivating the heart-mind and its various forms of intelligence through attention and attitude transformation practices.

In the *Dhammapada,* the collection of several hundred short quotes taken from the Buddha's original teachings, the Buddha says, "The mind is flighty and elusive, moving wherever it pleases. Taming it is wonderful indeed—for a disciplined mind invites true joy." He also said, "The mind is restless and cunning, difficult to calm, difficult to guard. As the archer makes his arrows straight, so the wise straighten out their minds." Nothing makes us happier than a satisfied mind; this is timeless wisdom. This is why it is always said that paradise, heaven, and nirvana lie *within.*

Learning to consciously direct, focus, and tame the flighty, restless, and confused mind is the heroic challenge of life; learning to understand and realize the ultimate nature of the flighty, restless, and elusive mind is the heroic task we all face.

There is an ancient teaching tale that is often used to illustrate concentration training and the nature of mind: Once upon a time in ancient India a saintly old holy man, a sadhu, was sitting by the wide stone steps leading down to the banks of the Ganges River in Benares. His pet monkey, in the meantime, was out of control. The monkey was frantically leaping about in an effort to amuse himself. The sadhu kept giving the monkey little tasks to perform as he sang his hymns to God. But the monkey could not be pacified. He wasn't content to merely play near his master as passersby dropped small coins into the sadhu's brass alms bowl.

Finally the sadhu asked his monkey, "Hanuman, what do you want? What is your problem?"

The monkey replied, "Master, I need to be occupied. I have infinite energy. I am at your service. Tell me what to do—any task at all, and I shall accomplish it to your satisfaction."

The sadhu replied: "Do you see that tall, straight, wooden flagpole standing there, near the gate to the riverside temple? While I remain seated here I want you to go, climb to the top of the pole. When you get there, come down again, and we'll talk."

After the monkey finished climbing up and down the pole, the sadhu said, "Now that you have shown me, your master, that you are able to do this task, begin going up and down that pole until I'm ready to leave."

In this way the monkey was fully occupied, if not gainfully employed. Thus he didn't disturb the sadhu, who renewed his devotional chants unhindered.

The monkey, of course is a metaphor for the attention and how the mind works. Meditation practice helps to train and concentrate our monkey-like mind, as in the sadhu story, so that, like a trained horse, the power of focused attention and awareness can be used however we choose, rather than it running us all around. Since everything depends on our mind, even more than on our body, cultivating a well-tamed, stable, and concentrated mind can bring us the serenity and spiritual realization we seek, as well as providing extraordinary feelings of bliss, infinite peace, harmony, and incandescent awareness.

BASIC MEDITATION PRACTICE

There is a joke in Buddhist circles: "Don't just do something, sit there." Meditation, of course, is how we train in continuous awareness. It is also how we train in letting go. Meditating might not appear to be very exciting or productive, but try it and give inner peace a chance. Meditation is a truly transformative spiritual exercise. Beginning meditators don't always connect the simplicity of what they are doing to the essence of the spiritual search, but it's all there to be discovered by those who try it. The Dzogchen teachings of Tibet say one moment of total awareness is one moment of perfect freedom and enlightenment. One need not seek elsewhere; it is all within. What we seek, we are.

When the Buddha instructed his students, he advised that they go to the forest or a solitary place in order to begin. By this he was suggesting that they begin their meditation practice in a place that is quiet and free of distractions. Meditators then and now are told to sit comfortably with their backs erect. They are instructed to stay alert and yet relaxed and at ease. This begins the training in mindfulness, or in cultivating heightened consciousness and awareness. The Bengali riverbank yogi master, Tilopa, sang:

> Still the body and relax.
> Shut the mouth and be silent.
> Calm and empty your mind,
> Like a hollow bamboo.
> > Do not give or take,
> Reach out or in.
> Leave your mind at rest.
> Remain unentangled by outer things
> Or inner feelings of bliss or emptiness.
> Thus you will reach enlightenment.

We begin breathing in and out through the nostrils. Mindfully, students of meditation breathe in, and mindfully we breathe out. We let go of the natural flow of energy and breathing, and learn to simply let it be. We pay close attention to each and every inhalation and exhalation, following the breath—the object of our attention all the way in and all the way out.

Breathe in through your nostrils, be acutely aware, and just let the breath go. Do this again and again. This is basic Buddhist meditation. What could be simpler or more natural? What could be more inspirational? Inspiring, expiring; inhaling and exhaling; giving and receiving; life and death. One great circle, ceaselessly flowing like waves. Pay attention! It pays off. Bare attention and nonjudgmental choiceless awareness enacts the practice of freedom through letting go. Letting go; letting be; being free.

Breath awareness practice may not seem immediately productive, but give it a chance. Some spiritual masters make it their primary practice throughout their entire lives. Mindfulness of breathing is the basic meditation practice, and yet it has the power to reach and enhance all levels of consciousness. It may appear simple, but even so it works on all levels of the path and is certainly not just for beginners.

It may not be immediately apparent, but to be totally in the moment, which is what meditation requires, means relinquishing the past, the future, and the dualism that makes a distinction between self and other. This is the essence of letting go.

We practice letting go by letting go of the breath again and again, experiencing a feeling of releasing and relaxing a little more with each outbreath. Each outbreath is a little death, a little relinquishing, a little dropping away. What a relief. Try it!

Like a plant whose roots take in groundwater, we sink our roots in the holy now, the eternal instant. In this way we can learn to draw spiritual sustenance from this very moment, right now. This is the only place to be, the best seat in the house. Take your seat, like a Buddha.

Take a deep breath in through your nostrils. Follow the outbreath. Ride it, ride the breath all the way out, out, out. Dissolve with it into thin air. As the breath dissolves into open space, our concepts, attachments, and clinging all release into infinite spacious awareness. Breath after breath, drop your attachments. Practice a little more letting go with each outbreath. Let go of a little more physical and mental tension with each delightful exhalation. In this way, ride the waves of breath, letting these sea-like waves wash through you and carry everything away.

If physical sensations or feelings arise, keep the attention on the breath. Ride the breath and let them slip away. If thoughts arise, as they will, simply breathe out and ride the breath all the way out, letting the thoughts also dissolve and pass away, as they will. Don't fall into chains of discursive thinking and analysis. Don't keep feeding and fueling the mental engines. Stay with bare awareness. Keep starting again with each breath, starting anew and afresh. Every moment is a new moment, like the dawn of creation. This moment is the only moment. Each breath is a fresh breath. Let go of the old. Make way for starting anew and you will be continuously renewed.

Breathing in, breathing out—rhythmic, like the waves of the sea. We are releasing, settling down and learning how to just be. Let things settle on their own, in their own time, their own way, their own place. Wherever things fall and land, let them fall into place as they will, without intervention or artifice. Learn to let things come and go; learn to just be. This is a huge step, an incandescent lesson.

This is the art and practice of freedom, the practice of letting go.

The wide-open expanse of the view,
The true condition of mind,
Is like the sky, like space:
Without center, without edge, without goal.

DZOGCHEN MASTER SHABKAR RINPOCHE,
trans. Matthieu Ricard

CHAPTER SIX

Healing the World, Healing Ourselves

Pray for the dead and fight like hell for the living.

MOTHER JONES

Last year I was at an AIDS demonstration when somebody handed me a lapel button with the above quotation. Mary Harris Jones, best known as Mother Jones, was a great American labor activist. She lived from 1837 to 1930 and is often described as "the grandmother of all agitators." Mother Jones lost her ironworker husband and their four children to yellow fever, but that didn't stop her from fighting for the rights of other workers and other children. Probably it further ignited her social conscience and inspired activism. She fought hard for those who worked in mines, factories, mills, on farms, and railroads. At the age of seventy-three, fighting for humane child labor laws, she organized a march from Philadelphia to New York to confront President Theodore Roosevelt; she hoped to raise his awareness of the millions of young children who were working adult jobs in horrific conditions throughout America. When she was in her eighties Mother Jones was arrested for organizing miners, and she continued fighting for laborers as long as she lived. She worked unstintingly to improve the lives of the men, women, and children who were building this country. Remember that she lived most of her long life in a time when women could not yet vote.

Thinking about the social involvement with which Mother Jones lived her life brought to mind many conversations that I had with my revered Tibetan teachers. These wise masters reminded their students time and time again that the Buddhist path is one of passionate care and concern for the world, those in it, and life itself.

Spiritual detachment and equanimity should never be equated with indifference or complacent resignation. I think this important because there are people who misunderstand Buddhism and believe that it emphasizes a kind of life-denying detachment or world-weariness. People whose encounters with Buddhism have been brief at best sometimes see statues of the meditating Buddha and assume that his peace and serenity means that a Buddhist, or aspiring Buddha, is no longer concerned with this planet and its inhabitants. Actually the Buddhist path is one that is in the world, but not of it. Even though the Buddha was free of attachment, he felt love and compassion for the world and its inhabitants. The Eastern image most often invoked is that of the lotus with its roots in the mud while it faces upward toward the sun and the heavens. In the world, yet above it all.

We don't often think of the Buddha as a social activist and reformer, but he was. He was the first major leader in history to provide equal opportunity for women and those bound by the caste system. He was an environmentalist who told his monks and nuns to plant a tree each year in order to replenish the resources they had used. He marched every day for peace and enlightenment, walking the streets of India, bringing his message door to door. There was at least one occasion when he even served as a peacekeeper between warring kingdoms.

The Buddha's long life of spiritual work and service is an example for all of us. Cultivating inner peace, equanimity, and an attitude of nonattachment doesn't mean giving in to complacency and indifference. It doesn't mean turning our backs on the suffering, poverty, sickness, and injustice in the world. And it doesn't mean giving up on the joy and delights of life itself. Living is a precious opportunity, not to be squandered. Life is a miracle, a gift; it must be cherished and protected. Tibetan Buddhists call it "precious human life." We Buddhists believe that a better world, whether it's called an enlightened life or nirvana itself, is right here and can be found within this world.

A man I liked, but didn't know well, died last year. Avram was an ultra-Orthodox Talmudic scholar, a gentle man much loved by his friends and family. He was also still relatively young, only in his forties. In the last years of his life, he fought nobly against death. When he was first diagnosed with a rare and inoperable form of cancer, he quickly became proficient on a computer in order to research possible treatments for his disease. Then, when traditional medicine gave up on him, he visited alternative practitioners and tried a whole range of remedies in the hope that he would live. Finally he went on a strict diet—no wheat, dairy, or sugar. Mostly he ate salads and raw fruits and vegetables. With his typical good humor, he said that at least it "simplified the whole business of keeping kosher." Avram believed that all these methods extended his life, and for a while, he felt quite good. But ultimately green leafy vegetables were no match for the deadly disease.

Avram said that he wasn't afraid of death, but he worried about his wife and five children. Two of his sons had yet to be Bar Mitzvahed. His daughter had only turned fourteen. His wife was afraid to be without him. In the weeks before he died, the wise and holy men of his community gathered together to pray and discuss what could yet be done. They didn't want to give up on Avram. They wanted and needed a miracle. As a religion, Judaism has always put a great deal of importance on an individual's name. It is a custom, for example, among Eastern European Jews to make certain that newborns are not given a name that belongs to another living family member. This is done to make sure that the Angel of Death doesn't confuse the infant with an older person and mistakenly take the wrong one. In the same way, the name of an individual who is gravely ill is sometimes changed in order to try to fool the Angel of Death. A week before Avram's death, several of the most learned rabbis in the community came to Avram's bedside to ask him to change his name. This he did. But despite all these efforts, Avram died.

Avram's death might make some people wonder whether his efforts were in vain. They might wonder whether he was misguided in having such a strong belief in God; they might wonder whether he was right in spending so much time in religious study and prayer. But Avram and his family didn't feel that way. They felt that everything that he did and everything that happened only strengthened his faith and certainty in the life choices he had made. They believed that his conscious struggle lengthened his life, helped him come into congruence with eternity, and helped him prepare his family for his death. They believed that when he died, he was ready for the next step in his journey. It's not fair to say that all his efforts didn't work, because he had a good death. He experienced soul healing even though his body wore out. This is a spiritual accomplishment.

Over the years I've known many Buddhist masters and teachers. There is probably no group more fearless in the face of death. Tibetan practitioners regularly prepare for death. Yet this does not mean that they are fatalistic or negative about life. These spiritually developed and enlightened men and women go for medical treatment, both ancient and modern, as well as practicing healing prayers, visualization, and mantras. Longevity practices, path-clearing and obstacle-removing prayers, and healing empowerments are commonplace among Tibetans. But so are traditional medical efforts.

I've actually heard new students of Buddhism ask questions like, "Well, if everything is a dream, then it doesn't matter what I do, does it?"

The answer I always give is, "Yes, everything is like a dream. Therefore it's up to us to make this dream positive, wholesome, and life-affirming." We are in charge of our dreams. We have choices, and we can make a difference. We can change our fate; we can have an effect on the fate of others and of this world. We are powerful beyond belief and contain inexhaustible inner resources. Nothing is fixed; everything is possible. We need to remember this, particularly when we are feeling hopeless and depressed or believe that fate is somehow working against us.

Some people believe that everything is predetermined and that the hand of the divine is personally involved in shaping every moment. Others believe in nothing and see no evidence of God-like intervention. The centuries' old argument of free will versus determinism is one of the baseline discussions of Western philosophy. Do we live in a causal or accidental universe? Do we matter? Is my life meaningful?

Here in the West, many have believed our lives are already scripted; we have only to follow destiny as it has been laid out for us. This predetermined destiny scenario is known as determinism. New students of Buddhism sometimes express their own variation of determinism. I see it at least once a week when a young person approaches me with a personal problem, usually of the "I'm having a relationship crisis" variety. Inevitably before I can even begin to say anything, this person states, "Well, of course I know I'm having this problem because of some karma from a previous lifetime." This thinking reflects a simplistic sit-com approach to the profound teachings of cause and effect.

The opposite extreme of determinism is a belief that we have total free will and that we are responsible for everything that happens to us. There have been several pseudo-psychological mind-training techniques popular here in the West that expound this point of view. At its most extreme, this approach blames the victim as in, "It's your fault that the car jumped the sidewalk and hit you because you CHOSE to be standing in that place at that time." Or, "Why did you want to get sick?" As if we are so totally conscious that we are aware of everything from causes and origins to results and consequences.

Buddhism perceives a middle way between these two extremes. While lecturing at Columbia University in the fifties, Zen master D. T. Suzuki said, "The argument between free will and determinism can be better understood by observing my own elbow joint. Yes, it is true that I can flex it however I want—and I demonstrate, like so—but it only moves one way!"

We do have a high degree of free will and choice, which gives us a God-like control of our destiny; it makes us divine, creative, and proactive. Even if our own condition—as well as society's habits and conventions—were not an issue, we would still be limited and able to operate only within universal principles and cosmic law. For example, we can choose to plant the right seeds in the right seasons in the correct climate in order to get a fruitful harvest, or we can choose to ignore human experience of nature's patterns and take our chances on what we randomly sow and the sort of harvest we shall reap. That is up to us.

We all have certain desired and undesired outcomes related to whatever possible course and attitude we take in life, whether it be at the larger macro (what shall I do with the rest of my life) scale or at the micro level (as in, what route shall I take to work this morning). These include all the myriad choices we make each hour and each day. These choices determine our karma and our destiny. It's no accident nor any great mystery how this evolves, although one would have to be utterly omniscient to understand all the many gross and subtle interconnections and causative links that determine happenings and outcomes.

The ineluctable law of karma suggests that action effects results. This makes it clear that one can skillfully manage both energies and behavior. This implies that, caught between free will and determinism, we ourselves hold the steering wheels. Each thought, act, and deed truly does count, and significantly so. That is why Dharma teachings remind us that everything counts; the spiritual warrior known as a Bodhisattva is often enjoined to live not only morally, kindly, and wisely, but also impeccably, with fearless courage, precision, and dignity. Think about the role model the Dalai Lama presents as a spiritual activist in this world.

Buddhist teachers talk a great deal about letting go of ego-clinging and our overweaning attachment to a solipsistic view of the universe. That does not mean that we should let go of our commitment to life itself and its precious opportunity to further our spiritual evolution. That would be unconscionable. Life is too marvelous, too valuable to waste.

After one of my late teachers, the revered lama Dudjom Rinpoche, made the Tibetan refugee's journey from the high Himalayas to the humid low regions of India in 1959, he began to suffer from emphysema. It was a serious condition that stayed with him for the rest of his life. Because he had committed himself to work right here on earth, he hoped to live longer; he thus did whatever he could to fulfill that goal. He and his family availed themselves of modern medicine as well as traditional Asian healing techniques. Yes, he practiced esoteric longevity mantras, but that didn't deter him from utilizing oxygen tanks and breathing devices. He lived many more productive years than anyone expected before he died, in his eighties, next door to our Dzogchen retreat center in Southern France. His wife, an experienced practitioner, was if anything more committed to his physical well-being than he was. In Tibetan Buddhist terms, she was his "long-life consort." That term means more than life partner. It acknowledges the special goddess-like dakini qualities of a wife-practitioner who dedicates herself to Tantric psychophysical, spiritual, longevity practices. The time Dudjom Rinpoche gained in this world was dedicated to the welfare of others. The master's own life/body/energy is believed to be a vehicle to help deliver others along the path of enlightenment. Therefore it was incumbent upon him—not selfishly, but for the benefit of others—to preserve that sacred vehicle.

Dudjom Rinpoche accepted his karma, while doing whatever he could to work with it. And he did all this without being overly attached to the outcome of his efforts. As it says in the *Tao Te Ching:* "The master does his/her best and then let's go." Whatever happens, happens.

Buddhism has longevity and healing empowerments and practices that increase health and prolong life. When he was sixteen, the late great lama Khyentse Rinpoche began a seven-year retreat, living in a cave meditating and studying. Until he became very ill, he was happy living as a monk, but his own teachers worried about his failing health. His guru predicted that he would have a short life unless he took a suitable longevity consort, who was foretold to be a teenage woman living in a valley several days' walk away from Rinpoche's mountain sanctuary. Although he had no interest in marrying, he followed his teachers' instructions, found and married that girl, and eventually lived until his eighties.

My personal teacher Nyoshul Khenpo Rinpoche was also a monk and abbot-professor until he was about forty. After he experienced a near-fatal stroke, the elder lama of Bhutan told Khenpo he would live longer and overcome his obstacles to health if he married the devout Damcho Zangmo, who was the right consort for him, which he did. She helped care for him, and he thus gained another two and a half decades of life. Now his wife continues to maintain his shrine, library, works, and legacy.

Buddhist masters are typically very practical about taking whatever positive and wholesome steps are necessary to preserve and protect all life. This calls to mind a story, a teaching tale that I have heard in various ways in various countries. This is how I heard it in India.

Every summer there is a rainy season; some years there are huge monsoons that flood the Ganges. When that happens, whole towns go under water. Houses float dangerously down street and there is a great loss of human and animal life.

One year, a devout Brahmin was in his house when the flood-waters were approaching. The headman of the village came and said, "It's time to leave."

The Brahmin replied, "I trust in God alone. He will take care of me." And he refused to leave.

The waters got higher and higher. Finally some people came by in boats and asked him to leave. The Brahmin replied, "I trust in God alone. I don't need your boats."

By now, the Brahmin was sitting on the roof of his house. A log came bobbing along downstream with another Brahmin holding on for dear life. The second Brahmin said, "Jump, sir. Join me."

The first Brahmin replied, "I trust in God alone. God will save me."

Then a helicopter with some foreign aid workers came and hovered overhead, offering to drop a line. "Go away," the Brahmin said. "I can't touch your line because you are untouchables. Besides, I trust in God alone. He will save me."

Finally the Brahmin drowned. Shortly thereafter he appeared at the gates of heaven where he met one of the Hindu gods. "I prayed to you," he said. "Why didn't you help me?"

"What do you mean?" the god replied. "I sent you the headman of the village, but you were too arrogant. I sent people in boats, but you were too stubborn. I sent your fellow Brahmin on a log, but you were too foolish. I sent foreign aid workers, but you were too proud. What else could I do?"

The moral of this story is that it's very hard to see divine assistance in person; it is only visible in actions. Buddhists consider human life as a unique and precious opportunity that should be cherished and not squandered. Devoting it to spiritual evolution and a cause that is larger than oneself and beneficial to others is the best use of our time here on this planet. There is a world of difference between giving up and letting go. Giving up implies negative feelings of hopelessness or despair. In my own life I sometimes feel discouraged about my own work and efforts. I think, "Why bother?" "Who cares?" "It doesn't matter anyway." Whenever I have thoughts like these I take them as red flags warning me to beware of negativity and pessimism. Buddhism is a life-affirming, ethical, empowering, and hopeful psychological philosophy. It is well grounded in the present time. It is incorrect to think of it as a life-denying theology interested only in touting return—or ascendance—to other, purer planes.

Centuries ago, the great Japanese Zen Master Hakuin sang in

his renowned *Song of Zazen,* "This land where you stand is the Pure Land; this body is the body of Buddha." Doing the best you can, here and now, continues to be the Buddhist way. Letting go means letting come and go—letting be. It means coming to accept what can't be changed even while working for positive growth, change, and transformation. Letting be is a way of oneness and loving life in all its surprising forms. This is how we befriend ourselves and befriend the whole world.

It's not easy to stay positive and hopeful when everything is going wrong. There are times when everyone feels lost and discouraged. There are times when all of us feel as though we want to surrender, give in, and give up. When this happens in our lives, we need to realize that we need healing and rejuvenation. We need to do whatever we can to restore and reinvigorate ourselves. This is true whether the healing we require is physical or psychological. If physically ill, see a doctor; if experiencing psychological symptoms, see a therapist, psychiatrist, or cleric. Through it all, we can maintain faith and confidence in a spiritual outlook and practice. Prayer and contemplation can prove redemptive.

A few years back, I underwent my own little medical crisis in the form of a kidney stone. It felt somewhat like having a knife sticking in my side. At first I didn't know what I had; I thought it was stress or that perhaps I was eating the wrong thing. I wasn't particularly concerned. But what started as mild discomfort accelerated. Before it did, my lama Tulku Pema Wangyal Rinpoche called from France to say that he had a dream and there was something wrong in my lower back.

Tulku Pema's phone call motivated me to make an appointment with a doctor, for what, I wasn't sure. Several medical visits later, I went for an MRI and received my diagnosis. I did many traditional and nontraditional things to try to cure my problems. I visited doctors and acupuncturists. I tried diet, herbs, healers, and Chinese medicine. Eventually, although I continued to be careful about diet, I accepted that I needed to follow a traditional Western route: I was given two choices—surgery or lithotripsy, a modern medical procedure that uses soundwaves to break up and pulverize kidney stones. I chose the less invasive lithotripsy. It took several procedures before it finally worked, but eventually it did. I felt fortunate.

While I was undergoing all these various treatments, I was also doing Medicine Buddha practice along with other healing and longevity practices prescribed by my Tibetan master and the Nyingmapa Vajrajana traditions. The healing Medicine Buddha practice includes mantra chanting while visualizing oneself as the Medicine Buddha who holds a panaceaic herb in hand. In Tibetan medicine, one often also uses specially prescribed mineral pills, diets, and herbal treatments to promote longevity and enhance energy, happiness, and vitality. Other holistic methods are often used in Asian medicine, including acupressure, yoga, moxibustion, breathwork, diet, and massage. Tibetan Buddhism is unique among other Buddhist schools in emphasizing healing and in offering a complete yoga system.

Tibetan Buddhist medicine derives from the Four Ambrosial Medical Tantras. It is said that the Buddha himself, manifested as the Medicine Buddha, Bhaisajyaguru, in order to teach them. In the eighth century the King of Tibet convened one of history's first medical conferences in Lhasa, inviting physicians from all over the known world—Persia, India, Central Asia, China— some of whom stayed long in Tibet. Lhasa became known as the holistic capital of Asia, and Tibet was famed as the land of medicinal herbs, spiritual healers, and wise men, which became part of its historical significance and incredible mystique.

Occasionally people ask me: Isn't the desire to live longer, happier lives recognized in the light of enlightened vision to be selfish, materialistic, worldly, or shortsighted? Why are practices that help us be healthy and live longer lives seen as being spiritual? Buddhists believe that the spiritual heroes, known as Bodhisattvas, strive toward absolute truth and ultimate reality by realizing the unity of Buddha energy with everything that exists. They work to extend their valuable human existence to further develop and promote a spiritual end. This is not just for selfish purposes—as if simply to extend their own finite human lives. Their lives are especially valuable because they have unselfishly dedicated themselves to living for the benefit of others. As spiritual seekers, we all strive to develop this altruistic attitude and make optimal use of our ephemeral lives. With this purpose, whenever any of us take the Bodhisattva Vow, our lives are imbued with extra meaning. A Bodhisattva never gives up or descends into despair and hopelessness. A simple Bodhisattva Vow states:

> Sentient beings are numberless; I vow to liberate them.
> Delusions are inexhaustible; I vow to transcend them.
> Dharma teachings are boundless; I vow to master them.
> The Buddha's enlightened way is unsurpassable;
> I vow to embody it.
> For the ultimate benefit of all beings without
> exception, throughout this and all my lifetimes,
> I dedicate myself to the practice and realization
> of enlightenment until all beings together reach
> that goal.

The Dalai Lama himself has given the Bodhisattva Vow in this country and around the world. At public gatherings I have often heard him praying aloud in Tibetan. This passionate prayer, which is culled from Shantideva's classic, *The Path of the Bodhisattva,* epitomizes the involved and evolved attitude of Mahayana Buddhism. As you can see, the Dalai Lama isn't giving up his efforts.

> May all who are sick and ill
> Quickly be freed from their illness,
> And may every disease in the world
> Never occur again.

As long as space endures,
As long as there are beings to be found,
May I continue likewise to remain
To soothe the sufferings of all living things.

MEDICINE BUDDHA PRACTICE: HEALING THE ROOTS OF SUFFERING

When positive or joyous feelings and attitudes pass through each organ and circulate throughout our whole system, our physical and chemical energies are transformed and balanced.

TARTHANG TULKU

In Buddhism it is taught that everything has the power to heal and cure. That means that anything we encounter in our lifetimes can serve as beneficial medicine. This is an important concept because it reminds us that so often our well-being is in our own hands. We can use our environment and our world to help us heal our hearts and restore our health. We can be healed by words; we can be healed by relationships; we can be healed by medication; we can be healed by diet; we can be healed by friends; we can be healed by touch and massage; we can be healed by nature. Crystals have healing properties as does music. Prayer helps us heal and visualizations help us heal. Studies have shown that our animals and pets help us heal and shorten recovery periods. We can be healed by everything we touch and everything that touches us. We are all healers; we can learn to heal ourselves; we can help in the healing of others. Healing energy takes place through an agency far greater than, yet immanent in, each of us.

The healing mantra of the Medicine Buddha is:

TA-YA-TA OM BEKANZÉ BEKANZÉ MAHABEKANZÉ
RADZA SUMUD-GATÉ SOHA

The original mantra, like the original text, was in Sanskrit, the ancient language of India; the syllables can be slightly different, or pronounced differently, depending upon location and lineage. The pronunciation and form of the above mantra is the one I was taught by Dudjom Rinpoche. Whatever the language or dialect, it is the mantra of the Buddha appearing in the form of the healing master. Roughly translated, it says: "Oh healing Buddha, reliever of all suffering, relieve my pain and all suffering. Relieve the roots of suffering. So be it!"

I have often chanted this mantra for healing others as well as myself. It helped me a great deal when I had several bouts of hepatitis in Kathmandu in the early seventies. In monasteries in the Himalayas and in our cloistered retreat in France, we'd often be asked to chant large numbers of times to help heal a specific person or a group of people who were afflicted by suffering. Soon after I first arrived in the Himalayas I made a vow to stay in retreat for a month. I was in Kathmandu Valley near my lama's Kopan Monastery, living alone in a thatched hut with a mud floor. Sometimes my diet was raw corn from the fields and spring water from a village well. I became quite ill; since I had vowed to stay alone in solitary retreat, there was no medical attention. I remember chanting this healing mantra combined with the Tantric visualizations and meditative absorptions that went with it. I believed then and still believe now that this practice was instrumental to my well-being and recovery.

When I was in retreat in France, a friend's father was dying of cancer; the doctors had used chemotherapy and were not optimistic about long-term survival. Dilgo Khyentse Rinpoche transmitted the Healing Buddha and Longevity empowerment to him. My friend's father lived another ten years, which everyone attributed to Khyentse Rinpoche's spiritual and psychic intervention, although the patient himself was not totally convinced.

Buddhism teaches that all beings are endowed with innate Buddha-nature. Our only task is to realize it and to awaken to that which we already are. In this way we become free, perfect, whole, and complete. The concept of healing, both physical and mental, is important to Buddhism. One of the historical meanings of the word *Dharma,* often used to refer to Buddhist teachings, is "that which heals." The Buddha frequently made analogies to disease and healing to explain various facets of his teaching. In the original schools of Buddhism, the enlightened teacher known as Gautama Buddha was often called the Supreme Physician. His teaching, the liberating Dharma, was called the Supreme Medicine, and the Sangha (the spiritual community) was called the Supreme Nurturers. The Buddha once said, "I am one physician without peer." This teacher cures us from the ravages of disquiet and disease, aging and death, bringing us to a better life. Enlightenment is the highest healing. Wisdom is the ultimate medicine.

Buddhists believe that healing, like illness, comes essentially from the mind, not the body. Buddhist healing, therefore, begins with an exploration of the nature of mind and the body-energy-spirit-mind interaction. Buddhists recognize the cause of disease in the imbalance that exists in the world and in ourselves. The ultimate healing and restoration to the natural state of perfection (both inner and outer) is found through spiritual realization and enlightenment alone. Thus all types of wholesome practices—whether they be spiritual, emotional, physical, or psychic—work together to restore healthy energy and spirit. We may age and die, but there is more to our story than that. I have seen this to be true. Lama Thubten Yeshe, my first Tibetan teacher, used to say, "Illness is just a label. Death is just a concept." That took my breath away the first time I heard it as a young man. He said, "We have died so many times, I'm not afraid of it."

From the Buddhist point of view, physical healing alone addresses itself to symptoms rather than the more deeply rooted causes. If we don't heal our minds and our spirits, the disease may very well return, just as unhealthy behavior patterns and unfulfilling, ingrained habits perpetuate themselves and continue to afflict us, whether in this lifetime or beyond. In his fine book, *The Healing Power of the Mind,* Nyingmapa lama Tulku Thondup Rinpoche names the four healing powers of the mind: positive images, positive words, positive feelings, and positive beliefs. These inner qualities and their cultivation and development through meditation and attitude training can greatly strengthen our innate capacity to heal our mental, emotional, and physical afflictions.

Meditation, chants, and prayer in various forms are Buddhism's main healing techniques for they effectively transform the mind and the fundamental stratas of consciousness underlying and overarching our material existence. Faith and devotion as well as patient participation (through spiritual practice and ongoing resolve and motivation/intention) are seen as being important for successful healing. Buddhist healers teach that virtue, generosity, and prayer are also significant contributors to healing body and spirit.

The Medicine Buddha practice is normally taught and transmitted in our Tibetan Vajrayan lineage and tradition through an empowering initiation. It is certainly more difficult to learn such practices only through books, but these days many of us have access to the Internet, where one can find images as well as information about tapes, teaching videos, and CDs. There are books by learned Tibetan lamas such as Dr. Yeshe Dondon and Tulku Thondup. Dr. Trogawa Rinpoche has a medical institute in Nepal. Several lamas sometimes give more advanced teachings even in this country. Medicine Buddha practice finds its roots in the Lotus Sutra, which teaches that the Healing Buddha is equal to Sakyamuni, the historical Buddha himself.

Medicine Buddha practice is a visualization practice that can be used to encourage and promote the healing of oneself and others, and on several levels. To start, we get comfortable, preferably in a seated position with an erect back, but if it is necessary for you to be in a reclining position, that will work as well. Begin by breathing in and out through your nostrils. Get calm, get quiet, get centered.

Close your eyes and visualize the Medicine Buddha. This radiant Buddha is seated in a lotus position and in form resembles Shakyamuni, the Buddha image familiar to us all. The Medicine Buddha is a brilliant azure or sapphire blue. His right hand holds a panaceaic healing plant, myrobalan. It is as though he is offering the flowering plant to us. The fingers of his right hand touch the earth near his right knee. His left hand is on his lap in a meditation posture or mudra. It holds a monk's begging bowl that is filled with healing elixir poetically known as "the nectar of deathlessness." The Medicine Buddha is wearing the flowing saffron robes of a monk. If you have access to a computer and the Internet, you can probably find an image of the blue Medicine Buddha. He is also seen on the cover of such informative Dharma books as *In Search of the Medicine Buddha* by David Crow.

The Medicine Buddha symbolizes the perfection of total balance, internal and external harmony, and spiritual enlightenment. I was taught that the Medicine Buddha vowed to help us all enter the path of enlightenment and that he prayed for all forms of physical, mental, and psychological healing to be available to us through his intervention. This practice was extremely popular in the Lotus Sutra schools in central and eastern Asia.

Visualizing the Medicine Buddha invites the practitioner to enter into the realm of the paradisical Buddha Fields filled with the light emanating from all the luminous Buddhas. Everywhere there are Buddhas, millions and millions of brilliant Buddhas, radiant beyond description, beatific and blessed. Just imagining this heals my disquiet.

Now, breathe in and out through your nostrils and begin chanting the Medicine Buddha's healing mantra. Chant it again and again

TA-YA-TA OM BEKANZÉ BEKANZÉ MAHABEKANZÉ
RADZA SUMUD-GATÉ SOHA

Out of a radiant blue sky, visualize this transparent, translucent, rainbow-like Medicine Buddha figure—Sangyé Menla, as he is known in Tibetan—in front of you and raised slightly in the sky. He is sitting on a lotus, the symbol of purity; it rests on a lapis lazuli throne, symbolic of healing. Sangyé Menla is a gentle, peaceful, heartwarming, inspiring, faith-raising spiritual presence. He is radiating light from three chakras—forehead, throat, and heart. These three lights—white, red, and blue—are radiating into your three chakra centers in a process of mixing and intermingling. Sangyé Menla is transmitting and teaching you in a multitude of nonconceptual ways, on all levels—outer and inner, physical and mental, as well as secret and mystical. He can be visualized as a large image or as a smaller one that can enter those parts of your being that need healing. Use the visualized Buddha image like a focused, carefully directed laser of concentrated energy to purify, invigorate, and revitalize each particular spot.

When you are reciting the mantra and being illumined and irradiated, pray for purification, healing, empowerment, transformation, and the realization of enlightenment. Meanwhile the nectar-like elixir fills you and removes all ailments, disease, and imbalances. You are being cleansed and purified; all negativities and toxins, obscurations, illusions, and karmic imprints are burned and washed away by the brilliantly scintillating healing rays emanating and pouring forth from the blue Healing Buddha. Feel the blessed energy circulating between you, like a spiritual transmission, mingling with the beatific essential being symbollically represented by the blue Buddha image.

As you continue to chant the mantra of the Medicine Buddha, focus on your powerful wish and aspiration for enlightenment for all beings; let your compassion and aspirations for the healing of the suffering of all beings take wing and soar. For the benefit of one and all!

Continue chanting the mantra of the Medicine Buddha:

TA-YA-TA OM BEKANZÉ BEKANZÉ MAHABEKANZÉ
RADZA SUMUD-GATÉ SOHA

Let the form of the Medicine Buddha enter your being and soothe all your ailments, problems, and suffering. Let the light from the Medicine Buddha heal your inner conflicts and awaken your limitless pure energy. Experience the trust and faith you feel in the healing powers of the Buddha and of the sublime truth of the Dharma. Visualize the Medicine Buddha coming to rest in the parts of your body and spirit that are in specific need of healing and restoration. Let the Medicine Buddha rest in your heart, and let his rainbow light rays heal the places where you feel tired and worn.

Now, imagine that you, yourself, are the Medicine Buddha. Let his emotional, mental, and physical health suffuse your being with blissful harmony and delightful well-being. As you imagine that you are the Medicine Buddha, keep in mind that your innate Buddha-nature is always in you to be tapped and awakened. When you visualize yourself as the Medicine Buddha you are visualizing the awakened Buddha that resides in the core of your being; this is different than mere pretending, for the Medicine Buddha is always within you. Touch this innate radiance and use it to begin to heal and restore all that is inharmonious.

Continue chanting:

TA-YA-TA OM BEKANZÉ BEKANZÉ MAHABEKANZÉ
RADZA SUMUD-GATÉ SOHA

As the Medicine Buddha, let your boundless healing powers reach out to touch others who need healing. Take as long as you like to do this. Stretch yourself. Release the constrictions around your higher being. Experience the depth of your compassion and healing love reaching out to embrace anyone you know who needs healing; let it reach out to embrace all. Abide in that noble inner light, beyond any notion of inner and outer or self and others. Just chant, sing, pray:

TA-YA-TA OM BEKANZÉ BEKANZÉ MAHABEKANZÉ
RADZA SUMUD-GATÉ SOHA

CHAPTER SEVEN

Being Heroic in the

Face of Loss

Be kind, for everyone you meet is fighting a great battle.

PHILO

Philo, the early Jewish scholar, philosopher, and mystic, is sometimes referred to as the first theologian. He lived from approximately 30 B.C.E.–40 C.E. and appears to have spent most of his life in Alexandria, the ancient Egyptian city built by Alexander the Great. I love this timeless quote because it shows great empathy as well as undying truth. It is as valid now as it was back in the first century.

When we think about heroism, the mind quickly leaps to men and women who take physical risks to help others. But heroism is as much about inner strength as it is about acts of physical courage. The greatest heroes are often the quiet men and women who are simply and bravely facing up to the many unexpected losses and difficulties that life has to dish up. Don't we all know men and women who are being heroic on a daily basis? They don't think of themselves as heroes; instead, they tend to consider themselves "survivors" or merely people who are able to cope with difficult circumstances without running away. Facing doubt, conflict, and hesitation doesn't keep them from doing what needs to be done.

All heroes have at least one quality in common: They don't run away from their fears. Heroes are just as afraid as the rest of us, but they have learned how to confront and walk through their terrors. Quite simply, heroes aren't afraid of being afraid. When faced with difficulties, a true hero is able to make courageous choices and decisions. He or she is able to say: "This isn't necessarily what I want to do, but it's what I have to do." Heroes have learned to give themselves to life, even when there is no pleasure involved in doing so. Generosity of spirit is part of heroism; holding yourself back can impose all varieties of mind-made limitations.

Anyone who has experienced a major loss, whether that loss be the death of a loved one or the death of a long-cherished dream, is being asked to acknowledge and rely on an inner capacity for the heroic. Here are some day-by-day heroes.

~ At forty, Margaret is the primary caregiver for her nine-year-old son as well as her sixty-six-year-old mother, who is afflicted with Alzheimer's. Margaret is a widow; her husband died more than two years ago. Before she leaves for work every morning, Margaret first puts her son on a school bus and then makes certain that her mother is settled in the van that takes her to a local senior center that provides caretaking.

Margaret often feels alone and frightened by her many roles, duties, and responsibilities. She says that when she wakes up in the morning, she is usually gripped by several minutes of terror and depression. She hates going it alone and wishes she had a loving partner. She misses her late husband. She worries that her situation is such that nobody will ever want to share it. But for the most part Margaret focuses on the love she feels for her wonderful son. She remembers a time, not that long ago, when her mother was nurturing and giving, and she feels grateful that she had the experience of a caring parent. Margaret misses her husband most at night; that's when they would usually catch up on each other's day. But she thinks that she is fortunate that she had a good marriage for so many years and that her husband left her with some savings that supplement what she is able to earn. Margaret tries to be happy and find pleasure in the life she leads, and for the most part she is successful.

When Margaret was asked what, if anything, she sees as the most heroic challenge in her life, she answered, "Staying cheerful and optimistic."

~ Daniel is forty years old. He used to be a professional athlete who regularly began each day at the gym working out. Currently Daniel starts his morning by praying that he will have the energy to get to his part-time desk job. Daniel has been diagnosed with chronic fatigue syndrome. In the year immediately following his diagnosis, Daniel spent most of his time sleeping or staring at his television set. He says he often felt so tired that he didn't have the energy to eat dinner.

Daniel's wife has her own heroic challenge; she had to adjust to living with a husband who is unable to do anything around the house. Daniel's son also faces a heroic adjustment: He has a father who can no longer go out in the backyard and play ball or even drive him to sports events. When Daniel first got sick, he says that all he did was "sit around and whine to anyone who would listen." Then, after six months of feeling sorry for himself, he decided to deal with his loss constructively and became totally proactive about his illness. By doing extensive research on the Internet, he learned a great deal about the fibromyalgia that made it painful for him merely to walk from room to room. He became an expert on his disease as well as all the treatments, alternative and traditional, that were available. Recently Daniel found a doctor with a track record of helping others with his condition and began to follow a strict regimen of diet and prescribed supplements, and he is feeling a little better, and even more important, he is finding reason for hope.

Daniel often becomes frightened and frustrated. He is worried about becoming totally dependent on his family; he is scared that he might have to spend the rest of his life in bed. Sometimes his thoughts are so dark that he is terrified. What does Daniel see as his most heroic challenge? Not becoming enraged by people who believe that his illness is merely psychosomatic and "all in his mind."

~ Chris was diagnosed as schizophrenic when he was fifteen. Now, at thirty-one, he is in grad school training to be a social worker. In between, he has been in and out of dozens of psychiatrists' offices and been prescribed more medication than most people can imagine. Currently, he is on four different kinds of medication. When Chris graduates, he plans to use his skills and knowledge to help other people who share his illness. Chris is a concrete example of someone who has been able to transform his own suffering into compassion.

Chris knows that balance is important in everyone's life. It's essential to his. He is very careful about diet and exercise and doesn't allow himself to become overtired or stressed. In his early twenties, he briefly stopped taking his medication and ended up being hospitalized for months, which is a lesson Chris very much doesn't need to repeat. He is very conscious of the precipitating events and moods that exacerbate his illness and vigilantly monitors his well-being.

Chris says that his biggest challenge is staying in touch with his emotional and mental fragility. "When things are going well," he says, "it's easy to forget how bad it can get. I've got to watch myself all the time. I can never afford to take my mental health for granted. Skipping my meds is not a realistic option."

～ Tonight Naomi is going on a blind date. She's very, very frightened. A year and a half ago, Naomi was engaged to a man she had known since adolescence; she was deeply in love. Then precipitously, with no warning, a week before the wedding, Naomi's fiancé decided that their relationship was "stale." Not only did he back out of the wedding, he turned around and married someone else—a woman he had known for only a few months. This put Naomi in shock; she couldn't stop crying. Not only did she feel embarrassed in front of her family and friends, she felt as if her life and her ability to trust were shattered.

Nonetheless, Naomi doesn't want to spend the rest of her life crying over "what might have been." She wants to get on with the serious business of living. Although she is terrified of risking her heart again, she knows that this is exactly what she is going to have to do. She is being very brave in resisting the temptation to contract and withdraw into bitterness.

These people have all been thrust into situations in which they had a clear-cut choice. They could be heroic and determined or they could fold. They chose to stand up and fight. Look around. I'm sure you know people struggling with cancer, HIV, heart disease, Alzheimer's, asthma, arthritis, and other painful and scary illnesses. I'm sure you know men and women who are burdened with romantic problems, financial problems, family dilemmas, and caretaking issues. I'm sure you know people who have lost loved ones, and I'm sure you know people coping with depression and bipolar disorder. When the Buddha said that life was filled with suffering, he wasn't just whistling Dixie. The Buddha wasn't being pessimistic and nihilistic. He was being realistic and facing the facts. We too need to see these things as they are, not as we would want them to be while drowning in the river of denial.

We are inspired by those who are able to live heroically. Think about Stephen Hawking, the brilliant physicist who continues to make a difference even without the use of his body or even his voice; the only part of his body he can move is his left hand. Think about Christopher Reeve, formerly a superman, addressing the world from his wheelchair, or Mohammed Ali serving as a peace ambassador despite advanced Parkinson's disease. Think about all the courageous men and women throughout history who have spoken the truth when they knew that their commitment to truth put them at great risk. These are real champions, heroes of the heart and torchbearers of the spirit.

YOU ARE THE HERO OF
YOUR OWN LIFE

*The hero ventures forth from the world of common day into
a region of supernatural wonder: fabulous forces are there
encountered, and a decisive victory is won; the hero
comes back from this mysterious adventure with
the power to bestow boons on his fellow man.*

JOSEPH CAMPBELL,
The Hero with a Thousand Faces

Walking the spiritual path is inevitably a heroic journey.

Right now, I'm sure that there are aspects of your own life that
are heroic. Sometimes just getting out of bed in the morning and
stumbling into the shower requires a hero's spirit. Trying to live
a meaningful life requires a brave heart. Whenever we try to act
in ways that correspond with our deepest values and beliefs, we
will, by definition, face major challenges. If we are awake and
aware enough to recognize help when we see it, we will also
receive aid in ways that we could not imagine. Sometimes we just
need to ask for help in order to get it.

God, Nirvana, Reality, Truth—these are all huge concepts
that can't be fully understood by those of us who are merely
human. It is simply impossible to define the mysteries of existence with two-word captions. No matter how lofty our goals,
it's probably wisest for us not to get lost thinking about Reality
with a capital R, or Delusion with a capital D, and instead focus
on looking at the difference between what is authentic or inau-
thentic in our own lives.

We begin to penetrate the larger concepts by being intentionally mindful about how we live out the day-to-day issues of our
own lives. How are we being called, and are we heeding our
deeper calls? In what ways are we being deceptive or truthful?

How are we being brave or cowardly? As seekers, we are climbing huge mountains, but we are climbing them step by step. This is how we explore our own relationship to the heroic, one step at a time. And each time we fall flat on our face, we manage to get up again one more time. All we have to do is keep on keeping on. This is the pilgrim's motto.

Taking risks in life is necessary if we want to change and grow. Most of the risks we are challenged to take are not physical. Often what we are risking are our feelings and emotions. It's necessary that we'll have to face some unexpected losses and disappointments along the way. My high school sports coach used to tell us: "No pain, no gain." This holds true in so many other aspects of life. It's spiritually heroic to face your fears and losses in constructive ways.

Doing "the right thing," the compassionate thing, the caring thing, the truthful thing, and the truth-in-love thing requires heroism. Look into your own life, and you will realize that you are presented with numerous opportunities to be both heroic and compassionate on a small scale. Everyday challenges may seem meaningless in the larger scheme of things, but they are ways of preparing ourselves for all the stuff that life throws at us. We need to do small things with great love, as Mother Teresa said.

When we face problems, it's heroic to pull on our boots, plunge in, and do what has to be done. I always remember a story about Penor Rinpoche, head lama of the large Palyul Monastery of eight hundred monks in the Tibetan refugee camp at Byalakuppe, in southern India. When the monastery's septic system became clogged and overflowed, none of the monastery's other inhabitants were strong willed or skillful enough to tackle the job. So the learned and spiritually accomplished head lama himself climbed down into the fetid cesspool with plumbing tools and reopened the pipes. People in that Tibetan refuge community still talk about that audacious act with awe.

Some people have incredible professions in which they get to help people in heroic fashion almost every day of the year. Firemen are the obvious examples. As a college student I remember watching two firemen plunge into a burning house in Buffalo, New York, to find the family dog, who could be heard barking inside, after reassuring the screaming occupants who had just escaped. It was a heartbreaking, terrifying scenario, from which all miraculously emerged unscathed. Nobody has ever experienced a house fire, no matter how small, without being aware of the remarkable efforts of firefighters, who seem almost always to be kind and compassionate as well as fearless and strong. This is as true of volunteer fire departments out in the boonies as it is in a large metropolitan area like New York City, whose firemen we have all come to hold in our hearts.

LEAPING INTO BURNING BUILDINGS
TO SAVE OURSELVES

We all recognize the traditional heroic archetypes of the brave soul rushing into a burning building to save someone else's life, but how about our own lives? Buddha often used the image of fire to define and describe the nature of human suffering and loss. Here in the West, fire is also a symbol of suffering most often associated with hell, as well as a symbol of purification and transformation. Many of us are uncomfortable with the fire-and-brimstone image because it seems punitive and puritanical. Yet fire in symbol and reality is an integral part of the history of humanity. Uncontrolled fire consumes and destroys everything it touches, while controlled fire is nurturing, bringing heat and warm food into our homes. Like pain and suffering, fire has two sides—destructive and constructive; it depends on how we relate to it—how we use it.

The Buddha used uncontrolled fire as a symbol because of its vivid representation of the unenlightened human condition. He often referred to his students as sons and daughters and used parables to represent them as children who needed to be saved from the burning houses of their confused lives. One of the Buddha's best-known early teachings on the nature of suffering is known as the Fire Sermon.

"Brothers," he said, "everything is burning. But what is it that is burning? . . . The eye is burning, visible forms are burning, visual consciousness is burning. . . . The nose is burning, odors are burning. . . . The tongue is burning, tangible things are burning, tactile consciousness is burning. . . . The mind is burning, consciousness of thought is burning. . . . Burning with what? Burning with the fire of lust, with the fire of hate, with the fire of delusion. I say it is burning with birth, aging, and death, with sorrow, with lamentations, with pains, with griefs, with despairs."

Buddhism teaches that we are the victims inside the inferno-like karmic houses we create for ourselves, but we are also the firemen and -women who are capable of making a difference. We have a choice; we can save ourselves from ourselves. What does that mean? We can rescue our heroic higher Self from our conflict-ridden and ego-driven limited self-concepts. We can save ourselves from self-preoccupation, narcissism, indolence, hedonism, and love of comfort. We can save our higher aspirations for spiritual growth and enlightenment from depression, skepticism, self-doubt, nihilism, dishonesty, anger, hatred, and pessimism. We can save our good hearts from being corrupted by greed, materialism, pride, and jealousy. But walking this path and putting out these fires is not easy. If it were, the streets would be filled with so many enlightened beings that we wouldn't need electricity for illumination.

The heroic path challenges us at every opportunity. That's why it's called heroic. Quenching the out-of-control fires in one's life takes enormous energy, commitment, and perseverance. Perhaps the best step any of us can take in this direction is to try to be as realistic as possible about what we are doing with our lives. If we want to honor the hero within, we have to stop applauding delusion and denial. We have to be honest about our negative habits and attitudes and the spurious stories we tell our-selves. We have to relinquish and renounce our egocentric, self-serving, and self-referential tendencies.

When we are going through our own problems, we need to stay mindful of the problems and suffering of others. Being aware of another's pain while we are experiencing our own is part of the spiritual challenge and promotes both inner growth and greatness of heart. Empathy is the root of compassion.

CHOD: BECOMING FEARLESS — A SPIRITUAL PRACTICE

Chod is a Tibetan word that means "cutting through." Chod is an ancient Tantric practice based on a simple and true premise: Cutting through our fears brings freedom and peace of mind. We can dispense with our fear by cutting through our attachment to self and ego. We all have habitual patterns of clinging to what we think of as desirable, good, and helpful; likewise, we fear and avoid what we think is undesirable, negative, and harmful. Chod is a training that helps us see that these patterns and feelings are largely subjective and that there is nothing to fear except fear itself, as FDR said. Namkhai Norbu Rinpoche and the American woman lama Tsultrim Allione, author of *Women of Wisdom,* are two fine contemporary teachers of this esoteric Vajrajana practice.

In the ancient Tibetan practice, the practitioner travels to a physical and/or mental place where his or her fears will be exac-erbated and pushed to the limit. Often this practice is done in the dead of night in a charnel ground or burial site such as a cemetery. The practitioner than visualizes the most terrifying kind of demons, ghosts, and gouls that can be imagined, creating an atmosphere of pure, unadulterated horror. Then, when the fears seem overwhelming, instead of following the natural instinct to flee, the practitioner fights those tendencies and takes his or her fears one step further.

Practitioners of Chod invite the shadow side and its terrors in. Instead of recoiling and running away in a self-protective reflex, they symbolically offer their bodies as food to the demons. They literally visualize their bodies being chopped up and all of their blood pouring into a cauldron made of the upturned skull of their own heads. This gory stew is then blessed, mystically transformed, sanctified, and ritualistically offered up to repay karmic debts and satisfy the demons' hunger. This practice encourages practitioners to regard adversity and suffering as friends. I find this truly works in very profound psychological ways.

This unique visualization practice originated in Tibet with an eleventh-century female yogini named Machig Labdron, who had received it from her Indian guru. I was originally trained in Chod in Darjeeling by the wise and learned lama Kalu Rinpoche, who went through it with me step by step. Although I thought it a strange and an incredibly esoteric ritual for a Jewish kid from Long Island, under my good lama's direction, I dutifully headed off to a burial ground to conjure up my personal demons and worst fears. I should add that in Asia, cemeteries take on an extra terror because they are usually filled with wild and frightening animals such as jackals, vultures, snakes, scorpions, and hyenas.

I went to a charnel ground for the practice of Chod a few dozen times in India and in Nepal. Several times I went to a place near a meat slaughterhouse where thousands of water buffalo bones were piled high in macabre pyramids. One night as I was chanting, the bones began to shift, move, and rattle about. I didn't think it was a ghost or demon, but I did imagine that some kind of huge rat or snake was making its way through the immense pile. I must admit I was scared out of my wits, although I somehow managed to keep chanting, praying, and practicing the somber meditation and visualization until dawn. Was I ever happy when that night ended!

I began the practice first with a meditation on love and compassion. Then I conjured up as many demons as I could image.

When I felt filled with terror, I followed Kalu Rinpoche's instructions and imagined all the blood in my body being drawn up and out of the top of my head. I imagined myself taking my freshly severed skull and offering it with my blood and body parts and all my possessions as a tasty stew to the demons. I imagined them chewing on me until they were finally satisfied. And then, to my amazement, my fears subsided. The demons of my inner defilement and delusions must have been pacified and satisfied. I felt peaceful, calm, and liberated, for there is nothing more liberating than freedom from fear. I can still reconnect with this breakthrough when I practice the Chod rite now. It provides direct access to nondual wisdom, beyond concepts.

Having said that, in the twenty-first century, I don't think any of us should be visiting cemeteries in the dead of night to face our demons. It simply isn't safe. Nor is it absolutely necessary. We don't need dangerous places to find our demons. Even back in the eleventh century, Machig taught that the origin of all our demons is the mind itself. So long as we hang on to a selfish self-centered ego, we are at the mercy of demons. The ancient teachings say that Chod cuts through our attachments; it cuts through our terrors and fears. One translation of Chod is "ego-slaying practice." I find this heavy, but true.

I believe we can update these ancient teachings and make them relevant to our lives. Without leaving our homes we can visit the personal places of terror that exist in our own mind. Here are some steps to help you "cut through" your fears.

Define Your Biggest Fears

What is it that you are afraid of? Who is it that you are afraid of? Be honest. What are you guarding, hiding, avoiding, or denying? Are you most afraid of death? Pain? Illness and disease? Public speaking? Wrinkles? Are you afraid of losing your job? Your house? Your spouse? An autocratic parent? Does one person have so much power in your life that you are totally afraid of what he or she thinks of you? Start out with only one fear. You can't cut through all of them at once, so don't try. Where you find your greatest fears, you'll find buried treasure deep below within your psyche.

Bring This One Large Fear to Mind in a Conscious, Honest, Self-Scrutinizing Manner

This large fear is a demon in your life, so you might as well face it and get to know it better. Analyze what it exactly is that causes you terror. Be very specific. If you are afraid of losing your job, for example, see if you can break your fears down. Are you afraid of losing money? Are you afraid of feelings of rejection?

Are you afraid of admitting defeat? Are you afraid of what your spouse, your parents, your children, your friends, your neighbors will say or think? What are you afraid it is? Are you afraid that you won't get another job and you'll end up living on the street? Are you afraid of the loss of status? Are you afraid of losing your community at work? Are you afraid of losing your job-related identity? Are you afraid that you won't know what to do with your time? Are you afraid of the process of hunting for another job? Are you afraid that you will have to give up a way of life? Afraid of disconnection, loneliness, boredom, meaninglessness?

Are you so profoundly afraid of being alone that it has crippled you or been instrumental in troubled decision-making? Many of our fears revolve around dependency issues. We want somebody else to face the demons for us. Are you clear about the ways this may be true in your life?

Experience Your Fears

Allow yourself some time to experience your worst fear. For just a few minutes, imagine a worst-case scenario and go there in your mind. Put yourself in that situation. Imagine it. Visualize it.

Tell yourself that this is what has happened. Don't run away from it. Don't panic. Don't avoid it. Face your fear; see what is unconsciously driving your habitual compensatory behaviors in an attempt to avoid the worst. Do this and you'll eventually have a new perspective, more freed-up energy, and a new lease on life.

When we feel fear, we typically want to run away or avoid the situation. These reactions can be wise and self-protective when the danger is real and physical. Sometimes, however, the fear is simply in our minds. I'm thinking, for example, of people who are afraid of such things as visiting hospitals, articulating their feelings, going to parties, or even committing themselves to a serious relationship.

If you are anxious about the possibility that you will end up alone, without a partner, for example, see if you can access this fear. Think about how you can construct a good and satisfying life on your own. The more we can train in learning to "hang in there" with our fears, even for the briefest of moments, the more we grow in breadth and depth. Training in this way helps us loosen our attachment to more excess baggage. In this way we open our hearts and allow the world to enter rather than walling it out, which is what we usually do with inappropriate defense mechanisms and irrational fears.

Be Willing to Experience Transformation of Your Fears

Too often our fears become nothing more than old familiar habits; they become little more than attachments. As young children, we may have been afraid of crossing the street or going into the basement alone. If, as adults, we hang on to these fears or replace them with ones that are similar, we remain stuck. If you have a fear that is paralyzing your growth, it is unlikely that it will be transformed until you are very firm in your resolve and intention to deal with it.

If you want to change and let go of the frightened and

dependent person you used to be, you have to do whatever is necessary to face your inappropriate, unnecessary, and outdated anxieties. Loosen your attachments to your current problems. Many things don't require mystical intervention. If you are afraid of your debts and financial problems, for example, see a financial advisor and take practical steps. If you are afraid because you are overly dependent on another person, analyze these issues either alone or with a counselor.

One woman I know didn't want to get a divorce from an unfaithful mate mainly because she was afraid to sleep alone in the house. When friends pointed out that she could get an alarm system, she was initially unconvinced. However, when she finally had one installed, she discovered that ninety percent of her fear disappeared. She could easily deal with the remaining ten percent.

The practice of Chod reminds us that many of our fears and anxieties have an irrational component that we can handle. I have a friend named Barbara who has a great many small phobias and anxieties. She says that when she first moved to New York City as a young woman, she was terrified of the subway. She hated the darkness of the tunnels, and the sense that there were creatures like rats scurrying about in the tunnels. Barbara worried about becoming stuck during a power failure. For the most part, she managed to avoid the subway for several years. She walked and took buses. In emergencies she took taxis, which were much too expensive and put a major burden on her finances.

Finally, Barbara was offered a very high paying job that she badly wanted. To get there, she had to take the subway. At the time she knew nothing about Chod or Tibetan Buddhism. Nonetheless, she instinctively developed her own practice to help her get over her fears. She says that the weekend before she agreed to take the job she wanted, she got on the New York City subway and vowed that she wouldn't get off until she had overcome her fears. She rode the E train, she rode the F train, she rode the 1, 2, and 3. All the while, in her mind she conjured up all of the things she was afraid of. She thought about death and rats and power failures. Finally, several hours later, she emerged from the dark tunnel. She had worn out her fears.

I have a friend who said that he was terrified of death until he was reluctantly present for the death of a beloved uncle. He didn't want to be in the hospital room; he wanted to go home and hide out until it was over with. But his mother insisted that he stay with her, and now he is grateful that he did. He said the entire experience was peaceful, and the room seemed to be filled with an aura of divine love; he lost his terror. Death became humanized, human-sized, and almost friendly.

In my own life, practicing Chod over the years has helped me realize that fears are nothing but attachments inflated into bogeymen. Like most people, when I confront something I fear, my initial tendency is to retract and contract; I want to avoid and suppress not only the things I fear, but also thoughts surrounding them. Over time I've learned that if we can muster up sufficient inner strength to face our fears, our energy becomes a lot freer and less tied up in unconstructive behavior patterns and mental contortions. Our emotions and energy can flow as they should according to our own authentic feeling and emotions.

On a personal level, I have discovered that things I found frightening when I was younger turned out not to have been so fearsome, not to mention dangerous, at all. For example, if I feared conflict with a friend, mate, or colleague, I might tend to evade the issue and brood on my fears. If I avoided confrontation, in a misguided attempt to be more harmonious and loving, it sometimes cost me more than gathering up the courage to just speak up and air things out, letting the chips fall where they may. Little fears, like those about having my wisdom teeth pulled or becoming ill in a foreign country, turned out not to have been as bad as I had anticipated. Larger fears, like commitment, marriage, growing older, and settling down, also turned out to be fertile ground for spiritual growth.

When we give in to our inappropriate fears, avoiding social

situations and experiences we irrationally consider undesirable and uncomfortable, often we are doing nothing more than indulging illusions and our deluded feelings of separateness. Allowing ourselves to experience what we fear can provide the opportunity to meet reality face to face, and in so doing to experience greater freedom, harmony, and oneness with the very things we until then avoided. Being one with one's karma and realizing the empty, illusory, and transitory nature of the objects of our fear delivers us beyond ourselves into a larger, brighter, and more empowered way of being in the world. This is the hero's way. This is our true way.

CHAPTER EIGHT

Mindful and Wise

Do not pursue the past.

Do not lose yourself in the future.

The past no longer is.

The future has not yet come.

Looking deeply at life as it is

in the very here and now,

the practitioner dwells

in stability and freedom.

We must be diligent today.

To wait until tomorrow is too late.

BUDDHA

How can we approach life with wisdom? How can we approach life with wisdom under all circumstances, no matter what complex crisis is swirling around us? How can we reduce the number of regrets we carry forward on our personal balance sheets? How can we see life with greater clarity? How can we be more in touch with who we are and what we are experiencing? How can we be more in touch with the world itself? If we were somehow able to ask these questions of the wise and all-knowing Buddha, in all likelihood his answer would be, "Practice mindfulness."

An early Buddhist scripture records that a student asked the Buddha: "What is it that smothers the world? What makes reality so hard to see? What would you say pollutes the world and threatens it the most?"

Buddha replied: "It is ignorance which smothers, and it is heedlessness and greed which make reality invisible. The hunger of desire pollutes and obscures the world, and the great source of fear is the pain of suffering."

The student went on. "In every direction, the rivers of desire are running. How can we dam them, and what will hold them back? What can we use to close the flood gates?"

Buddha said: "Any such river can be halted with the dam of mindful awareness. I call it the flood-stopper. With wisdom you can close the floodgates."

Mindfulness, which leads to wisdom, can help us stay centered no matter how many distracting or disturbing highs and lows come our way. The practice of mindfulness is unique in both its simplicity and its practicality. For example, Jennifer, who lives in New England, recently attended a Buddhist retreat where she was introduced to several mindfulness practices. In one of them, Jennifer was given three grapes and told to focus her total attention on chewing each grape, one by one. She was told to chew on each grape very, very carefully and very, very slowly. "Chew as much as a hundred times per grape," the instructor advised. This kind of chewing meditation is part of traditional Buddhist mindfulness training. It can be done with any kind of food and is often practiced with a solitary raisin or a slice of tangerine.

Chewing meditation is an ancient form of awareness practice. We take the grape and we consider it carefully. As it sits in the palm of the hand, we notice its shape and its weight. We pay attention to the grape's color and smell. Is it a green grape? A red grape? A purple grape? In the book *The Color Purple*, author Alice Walker wrote, "I think it pisses God off if you walk by the color purple in a field somewhere and don't notice it." This remarkable sentence is Walker's earthy reminder to notice the splendor and beauty that surround us. The grape to which we are directing our attention is amazing. Be mindful; pay more attention to it, and you'll become accustomed to paying more attention to life.

We begin chewing the grape with great care. We don't swallow. We let go of everything else in our minds and focus only on the grape. We are doing only what we are doing: We are chewing on a grape. So simple. We pay attention to the grape's flavor and the texture. We pay attention to the subtle and not so subtle differences between the pulp of the grape and its chewier skin. Does the grape have seeds? Do they add a bitter note to an otherwise sweet experience? As we continue to chew, we bring all of our faculties of mindfulness to the experience. Notice whatever comes up in your mind in relation to the grape. Notice what comes up and let it go. Be there, with the grape. Be aware of what you are experiencing. Be conscious; be awake. Awakefulness is wisdom.

We want to be able to approach life with the same awareness and focus with which we are now approaching this grape. Can we do this? Can we pay that much attention? Can we mindfully experience our lives? Can we know what we are doing as we are doing it? Can we wipe away the cobwebs and see the truth? Can we live life in the present moment? Can we be fully awake and aware? Can we see things as they really are and not just as we would like them to be?

Wisdom is knowing what is true; it is knowing what is real. To be wise is to be aware. All mindfulness exercises are training in the cultivation of attentive awareness. When we do something as simple as chew a grape with mindfulness, we are training in wisdom. We are in training to see things clearly without distortion or illusion. We are training to pay attention and to really see what is. That is enlightenment. So why can't most of us get there?

There is a wonderful Zen story about a monk who was promoted to the rank of teacher. Feeling proud of his accomplishments, the monk went to visit a Zen master. When he arrived he took off his wooden clogs and left them, along with his umbrella, at the front door. "Tell me," the master asked of the young teacher, "when you removed your shoes, did you place them to the left or the right of your umbrella?" Of course, the monk didn't remember. When he heard that question, he realized that he still had a lot to learn. Why wasn't he paying attention to his shoes as he removed them? What was he thinking about? Why wasn't he being attentive in that moment? As far as he had traveled on the path, he still had farther to go.

FAILURES OF MINDFULNESS

As we get out of bed each morning, most of us want to be present in our lives. We hope that we will be conscious and aware; we hope that we will be paying attention to where we are going and what we are doing. But in this modern world there is so much stimuli; we are pulled in so many different directions at once that it's difficult to stay focused and in the moment. Many of us personally experience this every morning when we turn on the computer. We want to get right to work, but there are such appealing invitations to read the news, answer e-mail, consider the ads flashing on the screen, find out the sports news, or see which movie grossed big at the box office. It's all too tempting. Distractions, large and small, pull us away from mindfulness. It's not that the distractions in and of themselves are bad or hurtful, it's just that we are drawn toward them almost as though we are unconscious children with no capacity for discernment. The great physicist Isaac Newton once wrote: "I do not know what I appear to the world, but to myself I appear to have been like a boy playing on the seashore and diverting myself by now and then finding another pebble or prettier shell than ordinary, while the great ocean of truth lay before me all undiscovered." I can certainly relate to that, can't you?

The ancient Greek epic poem *The Odyssey* tells the heroic story of Odysseus as he attempts to return to his wife and homeland after the Trojan War. The voyage is an arduous trip filled with dangers and temptations. As Odysseus makes plans to sail his ship past the sea rocks that are inhabited by seductive Sirens, the goddess Circe warns him that his life will be in danger because the Sirens will try to distract him. She tells him that they have the power to enchant those who draw near and pull them to their deaths. She informs Odysseus that there are "a great heap of dead men's bones lying all around." To avoid this fate, she advises Odysseus to put wax in the ears of his sailors. If Odysseus himself wants to hear the Sirens' song, Circe suggests that he should have his men lash him to the mast of the boat; he should instruct his sailors that no matter how much he pleads, they must not free him until the ship is well past the Sirens.

Odysseus tells his men of Circe's warning, saying, "I will therefore tell you about them, so that whether we live or die we may do so with our eyes open."

The two most important words in that quote from a Buddhist point of view, of course, are "eyes open." The underlying meaning of Circe's predictions warns us that we can all be tempted by the unconscious themes in our own lives. We are all vulnerable to the distracting songs of the various Sirens that appear in our paths. The practice of mindfulness teaches us to live with conscious awareness—open eyes—so that the less conscious parts of ourselves are thus illumined and the hold of the unconscious is thus tempered.

When we are mindful, we are less likely to get pulled into life's murkier waters or get dashed on the rocks. When we are mindful, we are less likely to find ourselves in situations where we contribute to our own mistakes and losses. How often in your own lifetime have you asked yourself, "What was I thinking?" as you pondered a recent mistake or loss. For example:

~ "What was I thinking?" Sharon wondered, as she looked at her dwindling financial statement. "What made me think that the stock market was going to continue going up and up?"

~ "What was I thinking?" Mark asked himself as he was trying to recover from a particularly disastrous relationship with a woman who could genuinely be described as "the runaway bride." "I knew about all the men she had rejected. The signs were all there that she was going to dump me too. Why wasn't I paying attention?"

~ "What were we thinking?" Frank and Georgia asked each other as they surveyed the damage the painting contractor had created in their house. "Why didn't we get references? Why didn't we stay closer to home and evaluate his progress? Why were we asleep at the switch of our lives?"

Having said that, I should point out that in my lifetime, like most of us, I have piled up a series of regrettable minor losses that are directly attributed to a lack of mindfulness. I remember years ago when I was in Woodstock, New York, helping build Tibetan monasteries and bring lamas to the United States. I was living in a garage-like studio that didn't have running water, let alone a washing machine. Once a week, usually on Saturday, I would head for the local laundromat on Main Street. The place had an additional attraction because one of my best friends told me that it was the best place to meet single mothers, although I must admit I never met any.

I didn't have many clothes, but I did have a favorite shirt. It was saffron colored and made of Indian cotton. I had purchased it in an Indian bazaar and brought it home with me. One Saturday, I was late getting out the door to go to the laundromat so I didn't get there until late in the afternoon. I didn't want to hang around because I hoped to get back to the monastery for chanting and prayers at five o'clock. I thought I would just put the laundry in a washing machine, leave, and come back to handle the dryer later. I looked for the sign that would tell me when the laundry closed, but the painted numbers on the door were so worn that I couldn't read them. There was no attendant either. So I took my chances.

I got involved in the chanting, and then I got involved with monastery dinner, and by the time I returned to the laundromat, it was closed. And of course, it was closed on Sunday. I remember thinking about my few clothes sitting there damp and getting sticky and mildewed, and it didn't make me happy. At the time, this shirt was among my most precious possessions. But life goes on. I figured I would get back to the laundromat first thing Monday morning, which is what I did. But when I arrived, there was still no attendant, no single moms, and also no laundry. I couldn't believe it. I looked through all the dryers and washing machines. I searched in corners, and banged on what appeared to be a locked door in the rear in the hopes that some mysterious laundry munchkin would emerge. I found the phone number for the person who ran the laundromat. "We're sorry," a voice said, "but there *is* a sign that says we are not responsible for clothes left in the laundromat."

"Do you have a lost and found?" I asked.

"No." There was no significant information forthcoming. They had a disclaimer on the wall. And I had lost my clothes.

The next day I ran into a buddy who happened to be a lawyer, and I asked him if there was anything I could do. I was again told no. He could call, but they would probably tell him exactly what they had told me. Besides, he doubted if they knew who had taken my laundry. And that was the end of it. My saffron shirt was gone, never to be found again. But I didn't let go if it so quickly. Whenever I was in the town of Woodstock, I would look around to see if anybody was wearing it. And if I were to be totally honest here, I would admit that the smallest part of my small mind is, years later, still looking for somebody wearing my shirt.

That shirt was lost through a combination of circumstances, not the least of which was my lack of mindfulness. I've chalked up a fair number of other losses like this over the years. Most of us have. My friend Judith recently threw away a full set of keys, and to make it worse, one of the keys on her chain was without a duplicate. Judith's lack of mindfulness ended up costing her valuable time and money. I have a friend whose wife makes him wear his house key on a brightly colored lanyard around his neck. She says she is tired of searching high and low, through closets, coats, and grass. I have another friend who drove to the beach one day and managed to lose his car keys in the sand.

We all have favorite little objects about which we regularly fail to be mindful—eyeglasses, cordless phones, and TV remotes come immediately to mind. These failures waste our time and annoy our housemates. Often they cost us money as well. One woman I know says that she has put her cordless phone down on the bed, and then followed it up by absentmindedly throwing the bedding and the phone into the washing machine more times than she cares to remember.

In what small ways do you personally fail to be mindful? Think about the Zen monk and his teacher's question about his shoes. Can we start to develop that level of mindful attention in our lives? Can we become aware of not just where we leave the keys or glasses or the remote control, but whether we are specifically placing "our shoes to the right or the left of the umbrella." Think about the level of clarity and attentive presence of mind that requires. Think about how awake and in control of our own minds we would be if we were able to be aware of everything we did. Think about the time, money, and emotional distress we would save ourselves. Our minds would be powerful beyond words.

In life, there are also times when our failure to be mindful ends up being far more destructive and upsetting. Think about any of the totally mindless and careless things you have done and the terrible consequences you have suffered or caused others to suffer. Joe, for example, can't stop blaming himself that his dog was hit by a car. Fortunately the dog survived and is walking, after painful surgery and follow-up treatment. Joe still feels guilty because he knows that if he had been paying attention, the dog would never have gotten out of the yard and into the street. Mindfulness is always the antidote to neglect and ignoring things.

Dawn says her failures of mindfulness are revealed in a series of bad life choices she made when she simply wasn't paying attention. For example: She bought an apartment in a neighborhood she didn't like; she started a relationship with a man she knew was married; and she took a job for a company she knew was having serious problems. In each one of these examples, Dawn knew she was probably making a mistake, but she didn't pay enough attention to warning signals. She is not the first person to describe herself as being unconscious and asleep. Don't we all sometimes feel as though we are sleepwalking through life?

Margot blames herself for the failure of her marriage. She knows that she was the one who worked late five nights a week and slept all weekend. She says, "I would walk through the door to the apartment, blow a kiss to my husband, and then phone

one of my friends for an extended conversation. I didn't pay any attention to him, and I didn't pay any attention to the marriage. I somehow thought it would take care of itself. What was I thinking?"

Don't we all sometimes fail to be mindful about the people we really love? Aren't we all sometimes careless about the way we handle our personal relationships? We vow that "next week" we will really begin to pay attention to the things and people that really matter, but too often "next week" never arrives. It is an old saw that we rarely, if ever, appreciate what we have till it is gone. Country music thrives on this unfortunate contradiction.

Taking things for granted is the opposite of the exquisitely appreciation-enhancing aspects of Buddhist mindfulness, which helps us perceive, intuit, and sense what we actually sense and feel what we actually feel. In this way we can be far more lucidly aware of and therefore in touch with our own thoughts and habitual patterns of mind and body. We can stop and smell the roses along our path since we are far more attuned to the fact that they are there, rather than just distractedly hurrying along the way to wherever we think we are going, projecting our thoughts toward that future goal. Life is much more than a mere to-do list.

Attentive mindfulness sees things as they are, beyond mere concepts and intellect. It also knows them as they appear, function, fit together, and pass on. This clear vision/clarity aspect of mindfulness recognizes the external patterns as well as the underlying principles that produce and characterize them.

Failures of mindfulness surround us. A couple of weeks ago I was listening to the radio in the car while I was driving, and there was a program about driving safety. One of the men being interviewed was recovering from a serious accident. "I don't know what happened," he said. "I leaned over to fiddle with the car radio, and the next thing I knew, I was in the ditch."

When we fail to practice mindfulness in daily life, we are, of course, being foolish. *Foolish* is the antonym of *wise*. It's the exact opposite of mindful. Wisdom is not illusion. Wisdom is the opposite of confusion and delusion. Mindfulness helps us settle into the essence of what is, just as it is, breath by breath, moment by moment—through the continuous application of clear seeing, using our innate capacity for choiceless awareness and unfabricated, bare attention. As we look at the world around us, with its highly charged distractions and temptations, mindfulness helps us practice discernment and discrimination.

Bodhidharma, the fifth-century sage who brought Zen Buddhism from India to China, once said: "Vision arises where mind and world meet. When the world and mind are both transparent, this is clear vision. And such understanding is true understanding."

Mindfulness training and meditation is a training for life. We train in being right there with whatever comes. With each breath, with each taste, with each little pain, we learn to be more with life rather than against it. The late great Tibetan lama Khyentse Rinpoche wrote: "The whole thrust of Buddha's teaching is to master the mind. If you master the mind, you will have mastery over body and speech, and your own and others' suffering. Mastery of the mind is achieved through constant awareness of all your thoughts and actions. Maintaining this constant mindfulness in the practice of tranquility and insight, you will eventually be able to sustain the recognition of wisdom even in the midst of ordinary activities and distractions. Mindfulness is thus the very basis, the cure for all samsaric afflictions."

Everyone knows what it feels like to be in a situation or environment that is so stressful that it's almost impossible to "think straight." That's when mindfulness comes in handy. Even when everything in our lives is going wrong, mindfulness helps us be calm and clear. It keeps us from being overcome and overwhelmed by all those oceanic waves of emotionality and confusion which, by definition, color and distort our perception. Paramahamsa Yogananda wrote: "By the practice of meditation you will find that you are carrying within your own heart a portable paradise."

My friend Barbara says that it was the practice of mindfulness that helped her handle the many problems that arose during her mother's final illness. She said, "Mindfulness helped me attend to what needed to be done, in the moment, and at the time. Whether it was making sure that my mother had a comforting breakfast that she was able to eat, or making sure that the nursing staff was adequately compensated, my training in mindfulness helped me stay in the moment. This was very comforting and grounding. I have few regrets or guilt about that time because, for the most part, I responded to what needed to be done appropriately. It also helped me slow down and find joy in those moments when my mother was lucid and loving."

The practice of mindfulness helps us be far more attentive, thus increasing our memory, attention span, focus, and balance. It helps us stay with our tasks and be far more concentrated and wholeheartedly absorbed in what we do. Being able to stay focused and present is an incredible skill. Meditators train in concentration by using the breath, a mantra, or a candle flame as an object to focus upon. It is not that different from athletes putting their full attention on balls they are trying to hit with golf clubs or bats. That's why some successful athletic coaches now have their teams train in meditation. This heightened level of focus can help anyone trying to do anything, from hitting a nail with a hammer to figuring out a complex mathematical problem.

Mindfulness helps us better inquire into the very fabric and nature of reality. It makes us better listeners and better communicators because it helps us be more sensitive and aware of others. It helps us to better connect to others. When our hearts and minds are still and quiet and clear enough, we can become so aware of others that we can almost see the pictures their thoughts are projecting, and we can better understand how and why they react as they do.

Mindfulness helps us remember and recall what we are doing while we are doing it. I call this *re*mindfulness. It increases our focus and concentration, thus helping develop enhanced performance through deeper recollectedness. This is one antidote to distractibility, scattered concentration, and diffused attention.

I think it's fair to say that mindfulness does what no one else can do for us: It literally saves and delivers us from ourselves—from our unconscious drives, anxieties, fears, and half-baked impulsive emotional and mental activities. When we are processing our losses, mindfulness helps us be more open; it helps keep us from contracting and hiding from life's problems. Mindfulness helps us feel the pain and have a direct perception of reality, and there is wisdom in that. There is wisdom in feeling what you feel. Mindfulness can help us be there and work through the stages of grief. Mindfulness also helps us see the beauty and joy that continue to surround us.

Wisdom is not information or knowledge, but rather the proper function of an uncanny and uncommon common sense, which knows what to do and how things are, as well as how they appear and function. Wisdom is highly appropriate functioning and discriminating discernment rather than something we get or always have or can describe with mere words and concepts.

In Buddhist and Hindu philosophy, wisdom is often called nonconceptual wisdom or transcendental wisdom—beyond this world and beyond the mind—because it is a larger perspective than mere intellectual knowledge and analytical reasoning.

WALKING THROUGH LIFE WITH PRECISION AND WISDOM

Wouldn't it be better for us if we were always aware of what we are doing? Wouldn't we be wiser if we knew where we were going? One of the best ways to cultivate precision, attention, and mindful awareness is through walking meditation. This can vastly enhance our consciousness and help develop our ability to bring meditative awareness, or mindfulness, into daily life. Who wants to be sleepwalking through our days? Putting the principles of meditation into action is how we become wiser. It's how we become conscious and awake. It's how we integrate Dharma into daily life.

Walking Meditation

We begin with standing, just standing.
Come into a relaxed state of pure presence by
   just standing.
Come into an awareness of standing.
Bring your attention,
like a spotlight,
to awareness of physical sensations in the body:
Be aware of the breath moving in and out.
Be aware of the feet and the sensations of contact
With the ground they stand on.
Bring your awareness toward
Being aware of whatever arises in the mind.
Mind the mind.
Remain more and more aware of whatever arises
   in the mind.
Be clearly aware of awareness itself.

Now take a step, mindfully.
Do it carefully, slowly, precisely, and conscientiously.
Take this step with full presence of mind.
Don't be absentminded, like a person just going
   through the motions.
You are training in wisdom.
Break down each moment (not unlike a breakdance).

Lift the right foot—heel first,
Then sole, then toe.
Move it forward
And place it down very carefully, attentively,
First the heel
Then the rest of the foot.
Begin lifting the heel of the left foot
Then the sole and then the toe.
Lift it.
Move it forward.
Place it down very carefully, attentively,
First the heel
Then the rest of the foot.

Thus the movement is broken down
Into lifting . . . placing . . . putting down
Again and again.
(To keep you on track while doing this, you may
say to yourself:
Lifting, moving forward, placing, putting down.)

It requires our total attention
While everything else is left alone
To go as it goes
And be as it is
In the perfection of things left just as they are.
This is walking meditation,
Meditation in motion.

Do this practice for ten minutes a day. Remember to stay in the moment and pay attention to every movement and everything you do. Let go of all other thoughts except walking with precision and care. Don't give in to the temptation to disperse your focused attention by straying into distraction. Stay with this simple mindfulness practice, cultivating recollectedness and concentration by just lifting, moving forward, placing, and putting down the foot—one foot at a time. Slowly traverse this joyous path of enlightenment.

As the masters say: "Hasten slowly, and you will soon arrive."

CHAPTER NINE

"Though Lovers Be Lost,
Love Shall Not"

Though lovers be lost, love shall not," is a line from the Dylan Thomas poem "And Death Shall Have No Dominion." It succinctly spells out a salient truth: That capital "L" Love itself is far greater and more profound than our human situation. Getting beyond the roller coaster of human emotions and tapping into that larger love is what we are striving for as we travel on the spiritual path. This can appear to be a formidable task. Saints like Gandhi, Mother Teresa, the Dalai Lama, St. Francis—men and women who have walked before us, and even among us— inspire us and help us see that this kind of love is possible.

When we lose people we love—and we will all lose people we love—seekers are immediately confronted by a spiritual conundrum: Even though our hearts are breaking, how can we search inward and continue to know and feel the love we all carry at our core? Being separated from those we love invites us to take a fresh and deeper look at the meaning of love itself. This is the major challenge of love.

Aren't we all a little terrified of loving another person too much? Aren't we all at least a little afraid that if we love too deeply, we will be unbearably hurt if the person leaves us? We all have some abandonment issues, and fears of disappointment, don't we? People do leave each other, don't they? We see it every day. People reject and abandon their partners; they choose to go their separate ways. People grow apart. Beloved children mature, leave home, and start their own lives. And, even worse, people die and leave grieving loved ones holding on to unfinished conversations and unfulfilled plans, hopes, and dreams.

Andrew Solomon, in *The Noonday Demon,* his fine book about depression, writes: "Depression is the flaw in love. To be creatures who love, we must be creatures who can despair at what we lose, and depression is the mechanism of despair."

A large percentage of the men and women suffering from reactive depression are doing so because they have lost loved ones. What feels worse than being separated from those who are precious to us? Partings are painful. Partings make us sad; they make us feel as though we are being beaten up by fate; sometimes they make us feel desperate and without real connections or roots. When we are torn away from those we love, we suffer from intense feelings of longing and loneliness. Volumes have been written about this condition. My mind goes to a well-known sixteenth-century poem that is as much a prayer of petition as anything else.

> Oh Western wind
> When wilt thou blow,
> That the small rain down can rain?
> Christ that my love were in my arms,
> And I in my bed again.

This poem is attributed to an anonymous writer, and I'm always saddened by the image of a bereft pilgrim soul wandering the English countryside, praying that his loneliness will be healed, and he will be reunited with the person to whom he is most attached. We can all identify with this prayer, can't we? Yet there is no getting around the fact that we will someday be separated from those we love, and when that happens, it is our attachment that will bring us pain and suffering.

Stories and myths about separation and accompanying longing are part of every culture and every belief system. In Japan, during the month of July they celebrate Tanabata, the Japanese Star Festival. This celebration commemorates the one night a year that Vega, the Weaver Star, and Altair, the Cowherd Star, are allowed to meet. According to legend, the girl known as the Weaver Star lived in the heavens, where she made beautiful cloth for her father, who was one of the gods. Initially the Weaver's father encouraged her love for the Cowherd boy, but soon she was so deeply enthralled that she forgot to perform her heavenly tasks. The herdsman also neglected his duties. Finally they were punished. They were placed millions of miles away from each other in the heavens, separated by the great Milky Way. But on one night a year, the two stars are allowed to cross over the Milky Way and meet again. In this way the fated duo share an eternal love—an eternal connection.

It's a beautifully romantic legend. We can all imagine the poignant longing these two lovers must have felt. However, as painful as longing is, it has a certain melodramatic appeal. We can become haunted by the intensity of the pain. We look through our mementos; we play sad music; we listen to country-western love songs; and we write poetry. Our daydreams become filled with fantasies that we are once again with those who were so precious to us. This is what it means to mourn. Processing grief is a tough task; it's all too easy to get stuck in our memories and our pain. Yet part of the healing is a realistic acceptance of loss. Life goes on. In fact, love goes on.

For some of us, it's also a sad fact that when we are pulled apart from those we love, we tend to transform our memories into the stuff of legend and myth. I have a friend whose parents had one of the longest and bitterest marriages I've ever seen. Her parents appeared to loathe, despise, and detest each other. The wife was particularly angry. When her husband came into the room, she couldn't contain herself: She would begin to hurl insults and recriminations in his direction. The most positive thing she ever said to her husband was, "That's just like you." When she said it, she had a sneer on her face. When they were apart from each other, they were lovely, friendly people. However, to be with them together was a painful experience.

Finally after forty-seven years of bickering, the husband died very suddenly in his sleep. Now his widow is beside herself. To hear her tell it, their union was one of bliss and devotion. She cries and wails that he was her best friend—the love of her life—and she doesn't know how she can continue without him. As bad as it was with him, she now feels it is far worse to be alone. And I guess, to be fair, they were devoted to each other in some peculiar way. Otherwise, why would they have stayed together? It's a fact that separation almost inevitably brings up feelings of nostalgia and longing. Absence makes the heart grow fonder; now, isn't that an original thought?

But this story does point out that as human beings, our feelings are changeable. When my friend Patti began crying that her husband was having an affair, her down-to-earth mother said, "You want faithful, marry a swan." We humans are much more inconsistent than the typical swan. People meet and at first they can't bear to be apart. A few years later they can't wait to sign the divorce decree and be done with it. And, given a little time, the very same people who swore that they would "never love again" are standing in line to get marriage licenses. Men and women find new partners and marry again, and again, ever hopeful even after several divorces. Sometimes they go back and marry the same partner that they divorced. I guess that divorce, like marriage, doesn't always work out. O, fickle heart!

Even when beloved partners have died, feelings heal and change. However, knowing that we will probably recover at least in part from the experience of losing love doesn't make separation any less painful or cruel an experience.

LOST LOVES

Don't we all have bittersweet and haunting memories of those we have loved and lost? In my case, the lost love of my youth was a Scottish woman named Suil. We met in India; it was the autumn of 1973 at Neem Karoli Baba's ashram, Kainchi, as it is called. Neem Karoli Baba had recently died so it was a very intense period for those of us who were gathered there. I was twenty-two; Suil was nineteen. We were both seeking wisdom, truth, and enlightenment. We parted soon after this first meeting and went on our separate pilgrim ways, but as fate would have it, Dharma and karma brought us together again in January 1974. That winter we independently traveled to Bodh Gaya near the Bodhi Tree, the very spot where the Buddha had been enlightened 2,500 years earlier.

When I was in Asia, like many others, I would try to spend at least part of every winter at Bodh Gaya studying with the many great teachers who would travel there on pilgrimage. In 1974 both Suil and I were at the Burmese Monastery to do a month-long silent meditation retreat with our teacher, U Goenka. In the days immediately following that retreat Suil and I got to know each other better. At that time several students of Neem Karoli Baba, including Ram Dass, were gathering ashram stories of our late guru. My American friend and spiritual brother Chaitanya and I were gathering them too. Suil, Chaitanya, and I started to cook and eat our main afternoon meal together. Before too long, much to Chaitanya's amazement, Suil and I were a couple.

At the end of that winter, Suil came back to Darjeeling with me to live near the monastery of my Tibetan lama, Kalu Rinpoche; Chaitanya went off to the huge Hindu Kumba Mela festival that occurs every twelve years in Allahabad, where millions of people meet on the banks of the holy Ganges River.

As that summer approached, Suil and I ran out of visas and money; we went to Nepal and lived in a mud hut amid the tall corn growing in the Kathmandu Valley. With some borrowed cash, we decided to travel to Japan to look for work that would allow us to come back to India. We arrived in Japan in September 1974 and got part-time jobs teaching English. We lived in Japan's lovely ancient cultural capital, Kyoto, where we could study Zen while we saved enough money to return to our teachers.

In the meantime, Suil and I heard of a Korean Zen master named Nine Mountains, who greatly interested us. When the college at which I was teaching had intersession, we traveled to Korea and stayed at his monastery. Meeting this great master especially moved Suil. We talked about him a great deal. We were having a nice time; I studied haiku with the American expatriate poet Cid Corman; that summer my parents came to visit, and Suil and I continued to make plans for our return to India in the fall. In the meantime Suil decided to undertake a long meditation retreat with her Zen master. Suil returned at the end of summer, only a few weeks before we were supposed to leave to go back to India. She had a shaved head and was wearing the gray robe of a Zen Buddhist nun. Ouch!

Suil told me her "great news": She had become a Zen nun and was going back to Korea, but she said that I shouldn't let that stop me from returning to Kalu Rinpoche in Nepal. What a shock! I considered Suil my sati, my spiritual partner, my soul mate. I was very young. What did I know about life and its comings and goings, its gathering and separations, and its plans and disappointments. As a Buddhist wise guy, recently deceased, said, "Sometimes life works best with no appointments, and hence no disappointments." But I guess I was counting on our joint plans, and I was heartbroken.

I thought about returning to Korea with Suil and becoming a Zen monk, but I knew it wasn't really for me. I wanted to return to my Tibetan teachers and practice with them in the Himalayas. I had spent a year working in Japan with that goal, all the while disregarding my parents' pleas to return to America. I had even missed my sister's wedding so that I wouldn't spend money. I asked Suil an important question: If I extended my teaching contract for another six months or a year, would she then come with me to India? She told me that she really couldn't say and she didn't want to keep me from pursuing the Dharma. We cried together. We were so much in love, but also so commited to our spiritual paths.

Suil and I told each other that we weren't really breaking up and that she would eventually rejoin me in India. In the meantime, we would each go deeper with our gurus into our spiritual life, and we would certainly get back together. I think we both really believed it. Need I tell you that it was not going to be? I still remember saying good-bye to Suil on the train platform in Kyoto, with many tears. We were both half-crazed, she in her gray nun's robes, me in my khaki safari vest and backpack. We spoke about our determination to follow our diverging paths and be rejoined later. Neither of us could know with any certainty that we were doing the right thing, but we both felt that we knew what we had to do. She couldn't in good faith veer from her path, and I couldn't wait in Japan with a formless agenda based on nothing but hope and expectation and no real assurance that she would come back. Otherwise I probably would have.

I left Tokyo for Hong Kong, went to Po Lin monastery on the top of the mountainous Lantau Island, and spent a week in retreat, preparing myself to go back to India and Kalu Rinpoche. I was thinking about Suil, while trying to let go a little and turn my thoughts toward the Dharma. I had to think a lot about our priorities and what was most important. We both had to come to grips with what it meant to put our spiritual practice before anything else. A few weeks later I made it back to Darjeeling, where I shaved my head and lived in a monastic retreat in a hermitage with Lama Norlha.

Suil and I managed to keep in contact during those years, despite the extraordinary unreliability of India's mail. Finally, I returned with Lama Norlha to New York as a translator and assistant in 1976 and went with him to Woodstock. I wrote and asked Suil if she wanted to join me there. She said she couldn't that year. It would be several years before she eventually came to the United States in 1980, traveling with her Zen master as his translator. In the meantime, my path had taken its own course: I was just about to go off to France on a three-year retreat with my Tibetan teachers. I remember bringing Suil and her teacher to visit my ginseng farm and the KTD Monastery. I remember sitting with her at the Zen monastery on the night before I was to leave for France. I remember looking at Suil knowing that this was another turning point, like the moment on the train platform in Kyoto. We made our choices as though they were foreordained. As I reflect in retrospect, it was as if we didn't even know we had a choice. Do I have any regrets? I don't think so. But I have to wonder about those turning points and how different life would have been if either of us had made different choices. For years my mother continued to ask me if I was still "carrying a candle" for Suil. Perhaps I was.

Ultimately, Suil and I found out that we were not meant to share the householders' life together. As Ram Dass said to me many years ago, "You two are together in the stars, but not in this world, in this life." Suil and I remain friends. Our relationship for me brought up many issues concerning the trials of holding on and letting go. I learned how to let go of what is not meant to be. I learned how to hold on tight when you can, and to let go light when you must. Sometimes you have to keep the love in your heart, but let the object of your affection go. This is something I had to learn about the hard way, as is so often the case.

Some men and women have a harder time with this lesson than others. I have met people who continue to obsess over old loves for years. These obsessions keep them from moving forward and loving again. They keep running old tapes in their heads and ruminating about what might have been. Sometimes it appears that these men and women are more attached to being obsessed than they were to the partners they have lost.

Often we can talk about the lost loves of our lives with a bit of humor and detachment. The relationships seemed so serious then, yet in retrospect we are astonished at the intensity of our remembered emotions. Perhaps we are even glad that these connections didn't work out. Why did we get so upset, we wonder, over something that so clearly wasn't meant to be? We are fortunate when we gain this distance. Some of us are even able to pick up the phone and call the lost loves of our youth, who with time have become friends. How truly fortunate we are when this happens. It is good not to leave loose ends dangling or too much mess in one's wake.

Others, however, have lost the loves of their life to death. There is no further contact. No more friendly chats, no more sharing of memories, no more plans for the future. How indescribably difficult this is to bear! How indescribably difficult to understand and accept! Many Tibetans are much more tolerant and accepting about life's losses and uncertainties than the average Westerner. Tibetans have experienced so much loss over the centuries and now, most intensely, with the loss of their homeland to the Chinese. I think we have something to learn from them and how their Buddhist faith has taught them, over time, these lessons.

A teaching tale that was repeated by my teacher, Nyoshul Khenpo Rinpoche, involved the mother of the renowned twelfth-century master, Jigten Sumgon, who was the founder of the Drikung Kagyu lineage. He was one of Tibet's most accomplished masters. I was told that when he was a young man he was leading a goat across the mountains; the goat was giving him a hard time, and he had to pull at the goat's tether with all his might. When Jigten Sumgon stepped back, his footprints left a visible impression in the rock itself, where it is said they remain to this day. The Lama was reportedly a precocious learner, a natural, a real heavyweight.

One day the erudite adult Jigten Sumgon was visiting his mother in Eastern Tibet when a close neighbor died. The heartbroken widow of the deceased came to the lama to ask him for advice, but before he could even begin to say anything, Jigten Sumgon's elderly mother started talking. Despite her son's eminence, she just had to speak. She had also known great sorrow; her own husband had died when her son was still a boy. They had so little money that the young Jigten Sumgon recited scriptures for pay to help feed the family. Jigten Sumgon's mother felt she had something important to contribute and share.

"I'm sorry, dear neighbor, for your loss," she said. "I understand how you feel. But this is what happens with all composite things. Don't take it to heart. Rather meditate on the inevitability of death and impermanence. In this way, from your present misfortunate, wisdom and serenity will eventually emerge. We shall all die; let's be grateful for this life we are given to live."

As the widow continued weeping and wailing, Jigten Sumgon's mother continued speaking. "Listen," she advised, "it's no use to dwell on your husband's death. Let your tears fall like rain now. But remember that this experience will soon pass, just like everything else. If you dwell on it, you will continue to suffer. I am rich with years, and life has taught me that it is best not to take anything to heart." The phrase *"Don't take it to heart,"* became a spiritual aphorism in that region for centuries to come.

The sad widow immediately began to know some consolation and peace. Despite her grief and sadness, she was able to reflect on the themes that Sumgon's mother suggested. In this way the bereft widow developed insight and wisdom into the nature of reality, and became a wise village elder herself.

All religions deal with the painful doubts and mysteries surrounding death by providing explanations about the afterlife or continuation of some kind. Some pose it as a kind of heaven where loved ones come together; others think of it as rebirth, reincarnation, life after life in which we will be able to complete our unfinished business with our significant others and learn more lessons on our evolutionary journey. We want this to be true. We feel so much love for the important people in our lives, and that love continues even though they are no longer with us. Isn't it said that love transcends death? Don't we feel that way?

I remember when my first guru, Neem Karoli Baba, died. I was in the States when I got a phone call. I returned to India for his cremation. I remember the love that existed in the group, the satsang, surrounding him. Of course I was too young to realize it at the time, but in retrospect I realize that I was beginning to experience the "greater guru" with the love in our spiritual family. Only the "small Maharaji," the frail human being, had died and turned to ashes; the guru principle and the guru-disciple relationship lived on. I remember singing the devotional songs all day; when I hear these same songs, even now, almost thirty years later, I am transported and feel as though I am in his presence, right in front of his feet. For me, he has never really died; he is still with me and in me. This is how the love connection can be greater than death.

Occasionally one hears stories from one of Neem Karoli Baba's disciples who claims to have seen him. Even in the last few years, the American minstrel Krishna Das tells me that he had a glimpse, a darshan, of Maharaji near a tree in India. Krishna Das was with his Indian mentor, and he told him to look quickly, but by the time they turned around again the figure was gone. Another friend swears that she saw Maharaji in London on a bus wearing a raincoat and carrying the plaid woolen blanket that he always wore in India. When she described what she saw, it was so vivid that I could imagine him in my mind's eye as well, on that London bus. These are miracles of love.

Miraculous visions, or darshan, can and do occur for some people. This is not unlike the visions people have of the Virgin Mary, or of other saints or angels. I myself don't invest too much in these mysterious phenomena, but many people do. If it brings them closer to what they seek, why not? If it's not fabricated or exploitative and it doesn't encourage an unrealistic attitude toward life, why not? Everything is possible; I have learned and seen enough to know that with certainty. Even without regular visions of my teachers, I know they are always with me. They often visit me in dreams, usually early in the morning. I know that Maharaji is always with me and we are never separate or apart. Love and devotion transcends separation and death.

Recently my personal mentor and Dzogchen teacher, Nyoshul Khenpo Rinpoche, passed away at our retreat center in Southern France. Yet I never feel a day, an hour, or maybe even a minute when he is not with me, just like my father, who passed away six years ago in New York City. He remains connected to me, mind to mind, heart to heart. We are of one mind and one spirit, even if his living body is no longer in this world. Recently I went back to his house in Bhutan to pay respects to his wife and his remains, and it felt just like visiting him.

LOVE'S CHALLENGE: LOVING IN THE MIDST OF LOSS

Some time back I spoke to a woman named Ruth whose forty-year-old son had died unexpectedly from some kind of heart fibrillation. He was just sitting on the couch. One minute he was there; the next he wasn't. Ruth had no time to prepare, no time to get ready for a loss of such magnitude. She said that after her son's death, one of the most difficult things about her mourning was that she found that she felt anger at all of her friends who had living children. She was enraged at them; she was angry with their children as well—for being alive. She didn't want to hear other people talk about their children; she didn't want to see parents with grown children. She only wanted to spend time with people who were childless. It would be understandable that hearing about her friends and their kids would remind her of her loss and make her feel sad. She expected that. She didn't expect to feel anger and rage.

Another man once told me that when his girlfriend left him, he couldn't bear looking at other couples on the street, in restaurants, or at the movies. It made him furious. He never felt anger at the woman who rejected him, but if he saw a couple holding hands on the street, he says that he often felt as though he wanted to slug them both. A rather strong reaction!

Loss can make us close down. It can make us feel as though our hearts are contracting—hardening as well as breaking. It can make us so depressed that there is no room for personal joy. We feel so bad and closed off that we are bitter and resentful when we see others who are feeling happy and joyful. This is a real problem when it happens. So how can we, as spiritual seekers, combat the bitterness and anger we might be inclined to feel when we are sad and depressed? How can we warm up and open our hearts when they feel as though they are cold and crushed? How can another person's happiness bring us joy when we feel as though there is no satisfaction in our own lives?

Buddhism teaches that everything springs from our intentions. The Dalai Lama often says that according to Mahayana Buddhism, everything depends on our motivation. Often the essential questions of the spiritual path revolve around our intentions: What do we truly want? Do we want to feel joy? Do we want to experience peace? Do we want to share happiness? Do we sincerely want others to be peaceful and content? Or do we just want to continue in our old unsatisfying ruts?

Psychology and philosophy remind us that there is another important word that is similar to *intention* and just as important. That word is *intentionality,* and psychology makes a distinction between intentions and intentionality. Here's how this works: Scott, for example, is chronically late for most of his appointments. His lateness has cost him three jobs and one marriage. If you were to ask Scott about his intentions concerning promptness, he would tell you that he really wants to get places on time. However, on another, deeper level, Scott's intentionality is at odds with his stated intentions. He is often angry and "gets back" at others by failing to appear on time. There are deep reasons why he sabotages himself and his work opportunities by failing to "show up" as promised. All of this has to do with his intentionality. One's stated intentions and one's intentionality thus can be quite different.

Our intentionality spells out our deepest commitment and wishes. As seekers who strive to follow the Bodhisattva path of working for the happiness and joy of all sentient beings, it's important that we try to be almost brutally honest with ourselves and practice conscientious self-inquiry to deepen our understanding of who we are, what we are doing, and why. We need to be in touch with both our stated intentions and our less obvious intentionality, our hidden and often subconscious motivations.

There are times when every one of us will feel battered and

beaten by losses; there are times when it seems almost impossible to maintain an open and loving heart. When that happens, one of the things we can do is pray. Prayer reaffirms our intentions and our wishes. Repeat a prayer often enough and it may even become part of our intentionality. Here's an example of such a prayer, from my own personal journey.

> May my heart stay open and loving even when I'm
>   feeling hurt and frayed.
> May I learn always to include others in love's vast
>   embrace.
> May my heart remain pure and kind amid the painful
>   details and muck of life.
> May virtue and serenity belong to all, even my competi-
>   tors and adversaries.
> May my brokenheartedness open my heart even further
>   (like open-heart surgery) and bring forth love and
>   openhearted compassion.

Make a resolution to start and end each day with a prayer for a pure and forgiving heart. At regular intervals throughout your day, stop to remind yourself to be forgiving, to let go of your attachment to anger, resentment, and bitterness, and keep the love in your heart. Remember to keep an open heart and to let go of an attachment to an ego-centered view of the world. This is the hard spiritual work that is intrinsic to the path to enlightenment.

Healing Light and Love Meditation

I like this meditation because it reconnects us to a realm of splendor that we often overlook. It can help us feel the love in our hearts even when we think it is no longer there.

I know some people think of the words *love* and *light* as being an anachronistic sixties holdover, but the concept of love and light is a perennial—an evergreen—far beyond any kind of fad or dated lingo. Radiance is an external symbol of the inner light, the deeper splendor of spirit underlying everything. This is an image common throughout the world's religions. Visualizing it helps us see it, become it, and be it.

At a deeper level, light, love, truth, the divine are all aspects of one luminous ground of being. This is where we all meet. In this, there is no inside and outside, no self and others, no separations, and no divisions between self and other. This inner incandescence lightens and enlightens each of us and the world. In this way we meet the world at the most intimate, loving level of heart and soul.

> Get comfortable.
> Sit.
> Relax.
> Breathe in and out, circulating breath and energy.
> Clear your mind and calm your body.
> Release your tensions, physical and mental.
> Enter the natural state of inner peace and relaxation.
> Imagine that you are breathing out all the negativities,
> All the sadness, all the pain, all the impurities and
> afflictions, ailments.
> Imagine that you are breathing in healing life force and
> energy.
> Breathe in healing invigorating love.
> Keep breathing in and out.
> In the most simple, natural way.
>
> Imagine a spiritual presence before and above you:
> A glowing sphere of white light, or a Buddha figure, or
> whatever image you associate with healing and renewal.
> Continue breathing in and out.

Exhale the negativities and release the shadows.

Breathe in the luminous light shower of blessings, wisdom,
and love.

Just continue to breathe out and breathe in, slowing and
glowing.

Imagine that every cell of your body is filling with this
glowing, healing light.

Experience your heart filling with blessings, love, energy,
and light.

Pray for blessings and receive love from that radiant image/
visualized presence.

Experience the rays of light entering and penetrating you,

Irradiating and suffusing you on every level.

Let the illusions and darkness of all kinds of negativity,
anger, impurity, ailments, mental hang-ups, emotional
conflicts, and physical infirmities clear away. Focus on
the part of you that feels most in need of healing love
and light. Let the energy come in, and negativity flow
out.

As your breathing circulates the healing energy,

Continue to receive blessings, inspiration, and energy
from that sacred power source before you.

Experience the relief of feeling unburdened and
lightened up.

Experience every cell of your body as being permeated
with a blissful radiance,

Warmed up and melted down

While being immensely suffused with light and delight,

With healing power and force.

Let the cosmic energy flow freely through you, liberating
you from all concepts and limiting constructs,

Beyond all separation.

Dissolve into that light/love/energy

And simply rest there in ineffable, pure radiance.

Now, share your healing with others by sending out
   visualized beams of light-rays from your healing heart
   to others.
Enfold and embrace them in your healing light.
Beam healing light from your loving heart
Directly to the specific problem areas of others.
Heal their anger, heal their negativity,
Heal their physical infirmities and emotional conflicts.
Experience the love and light in your heart as it shines
   out on others.
Realize the inseparability of self and others in the clear
   light of reality,
And rest in oneness beyond all names and concepts.

CHAPTER TEN

Spiritual Renewal—

Healing Our

Wounded Hearts

If you don't have the wound of a broken heart, how can you know you're alive? If you have no broken heart, how do you know who you are? Have been? Ever have been?

EDWARD ALBEE,
The Play About Baby

To one degree or another, we all have wounded hearts etched with at least a few of life's infinitely variant scars. But if that is the case, how can we find peace? How can we release our sorrow and move beyond negative memories and hurt? How can we alter and release our attachment to the past? How can we come unstuck? How can we let go of the person we used to be?

Men and women trying to recover from disappointment and loss tend to hear a wide variety of well-meaning advice. "You need healing," their friends tell them. "You need closure." "You need resolution." "Move on." Sometimes this facile, though well-intentioned advice, is the last thing that someone wants to hear. "Change your life." "Okay, sure. Will do. Thank you!" It is easier said than done, isn't it?

Almost twenty years ago, while I was in three-year meditation retreat, I received a letter from an old friend who told me that her talented and beloved son was gravely ill; he was only in his mid-twenties, and I remember being very saddened by this news. She asked if we would pray for him. Later I received word that he had died. I knew that my friend suffered grievously from the loss of her son. But I was still young and I probably didn't fully understand what she was experiencing. About two years later I visited her in upstate New York and gave her some platitudinous advice.

"Maybe it's time to let go and move on," I said.

"Maybe it isn't," she replied. "Maybe I'm not done."

The truth and authenticity of her statement were pretty startling in the face of my well-meaning, albeit useless, clichés. Maybe she wasn't done with her mourning; maybe she would never feel done. My dear old friend is not unique in her response to major loss. Many have told me that they have never really "gotten over" some of their experiences.

I once met a man who said that he felt as though his life had been nothing but a series of losses. "For me, there is no such thing as closure," he told me. "Some things are never over. Some wrongs will never be made right. Some feelings are never finished." I gave what he said a great deal of thought. We have only to look around us at all the men and women suffering from post-traumatic stress disorder to see real-life examples of people whose grief is not finished.

Mourning is a necessary process as well as a deep and significant spiritual experience. It brings us closer to the ground of our being and our felt sense of authenticity. We need to intelligently process our most difficult experiences in order to regain balance, harmony, and inner peace. But there comes a time when it is helpful to seek and find ways to release the pain. Yes, certain losses remain with us; they are part of our history and our karma. But that doesn't mean that it is appropriate for us to spend our lives grieving. We need to find ways to peacefully coexist with our sadness. We can embrace our pain and our losses and be greater and more authentically real for doing so.

I am not alone in saying that a broken heart is often the beginning of healing and renewal; many wiser men and women have spoken these words. Sometimes it is only desperation that can drive us out of a rut. When we are sad, we need comfort; we need to find new hope; we need spiritual renewal. These are attainable goals; these are all possible. Everything is possible to those who seek and persevere. In the New Testament, Jesus spoke the following beatitude, "Blessed are those who mourn, for they shall be comforted."

Yet many wonder how to find the comfort they need. How can we transform our own personal sorrows into meaningful growth and transformation? I wish I could tell you that I had a wealth of Tibetan "secrets" that would bring you instant liberation and total relief and protection from life's travails. But I don't, and I'm not sure anyone else does either. The spiritual path offers comfort, solace, and refuge, but it is a path—a process—and it takes time, willingness, and diligence. It is not a quick fix. There is no free lunch, karmically speaking. The spiritual path is a place to become more real; it's not a place where we can hide out and avoid or deny reality, or have others do our personal growth work for us. Unfortunately, no genuine enlightenment pill yet exists.

The fact is that life is tough for everybody, even spiritual seekers. I know that sometimes our lives can seem disappointing as well as less than we expected when we were growing up. But let's look at the other side of it. Are we ready to accept the truth that this world—this place where I am living now and where you are living now—is the kingdom that has been promised? When I was in France I had the opportunity to stay in a Roman Catholic hermitage and learn more about some of the Christian saints. Saint Catherine of Siena said, "Every step of the way to heaven is heaven." This is your heaven! This is my heaven! This is it! Overlook it at your peril.

We are never going to completely wipe out the memory of our grief and our losses, and probably we don't really want to. We don't want to become unconscious zombies devoid of meaningful memories and feelings. But we do want to find peace, harmony, and acceptance within the framework of our day-to-day world. Finding a way to peacefully coexist with life's losses takes courage, fortitude, and inner strength. The first time I heard the expression "Growing old is not for sissies," it was said by a beautiful woman in her early thirties who was working in a dental office. Looking at her one could hardly imagine that she was a breast cancer survivor who was still undergoing chemotherapy.

Each of us, of course, is grappling with our own karma. There is nothing else for us to do. Everything is karma. It's like the wind. Karma is the wind of outer and inner, material and mental conditioning. You can't control the wind, but how we sail and navigate with it is crucial. Just because the wind is coming from the northeast doesn't mean the sailboat always has to be blown the other way. If we are skillful sailors, we have choice. That's what is known as freedom. Here is a secret of spiritual mastery and deliverance: We can't control the winds of our karma and conditioning and the entire world around us, but we are in charge of how we relate to those winds, and that makes all the difference.

A life lesson that we all need to keep in mind: If you want your life experience to be different, you have to *do* something different. We have choices; we can consciously change the way we view the world. Change is going to happen anyway, no matter what we do. We might as well embrace the notion of change and find wisdom in the process. Otherwise, we are going to spend much of our lives resisting a process that is beyond our control. Change is our ally. Pythagoras said, "The world is a series of changes, sometimes in your favor and sometimes against you. When you are in charge, do good; when you are overruled, bear it." No one can genuinely flourish and grow in a healthy spiritual way as a control freak.

The fact that everything changes leaves much room for us to grow, transform, and renew ourselves. Change allows for constant regeneration and renewal. Most of the time, a life setback or crisis is the next step in the ongoing process of transformation. This is an important principle of inner growth and spiritual development.

Like most everyone else, I like to believe in miracles. I like to believe that some unseen being or presence is going to wave a magic wand and make us happily arrive exactly where we should be. But I know that personal change and renewal is more a practical than a mystical matter. The Buddha once said, "If you want to protect your feet from rocks and thorns, don't try to cover the whole world with leather; cover your own feet with shoes."

We all have intricate little nests of habits, behaviors, attitudes, opinions, stances, and preconceptions that could do with a little changing. When we start to let go of these, and in the process let go of who we used to be and who we think we used to be, we start to realize that whole new ways of seeing and being naturally flow into the space created by that relinquishment. This is an important concept to keep in mind.

Spiritual transformation and renewal are forms of healing, of rectification, of rebalancing. Such renewal restores us to wholeness and to peace through new beginnings. Our hopes, dreams, and aspirations are revived, and we are able to make fresh starts. Sometimes all we need to do to make a fresh start is to begin seriously questioning ourselves—our assumptions and beliefs and what we are doing. This kind of self-examination helps us think "outside the box." When we do this, it can help us view the world in such a different way that we are sometimes able to make dramatic changes. Seeing differently is believing differently and leads to different ways of living.

Buddhism teaches that the reason we are unhappy and experience difficulty is mainly due to ignorance and our false sense of incompleteness and separation. Out of this ignorance and feelings of separateness comes all kinds of unsatisfying unfulfilling behavior and effort. A pop example that comes to mind is the all too human tendency to look for love in all the wrong places. We do well to renew our outlook and our efforts toward more intelligent and fulfilling directions and modes of seeking what we really want and need. Remember that one definition of insanity is doing what we have always done and expecting different results.

Few of us carefully examine whether or not our current pattern of desires and habits are producing the results we want. Too often we just continue as we have always done—"same old, same old"—just as our friends, colleagues, and elders have always done, thought, reacted, hoped, and believed. We do this without thoroughly, conscientiously, and deeply scrutinizing for ourselves how well these strategies work for us.

Rebirth is one form of renewal and regeneration. This may happen in the afterlife or in heaven, or it may happen through reinventing oneself or one's career and relationships in this life. Or it can happen moment by moment by taking a good deep breath and taking a fresh and renewed look at life in the immediacy of the present moment. This moment-to-moment rebirth is a practice of both love and freedom. It allows us to embrace reality right now, as it is; it allows us to be as we are without being burdened or conditioned by the past.

When it comes to creating personal transformation, it helps to be practical as well as philosophical. Buddhism offers a wide range of ideas to help us radically alter the way we view reality and thus find peace and contentment even within this topsy-turvy world. Here are some consciousness-enhancing practices to help us change how we experience the world.

USING THE POWER OF MINDFULNESS TO REFRESH OUR SENSES AND RENEW OUR SOULS

Life is available only in the present moment. If you abandon the present moment you cannot live the moment of your daily life deeply. That is why those who are not capable of being there in the present moment, they don't really live their lives—they live like dead people, like the French writer Camus used to say. That is why if you know the techniques of mindful breathing, mindful walking, mindful smiling, you can bring your mind back to your body and you become truly alive at every moment and that can be described as the practice of resurrection. Resurrection can be at every moment for life to be truly possible.

THICH NHAT HANH

The cultivation of mindfulness is probably the most transformative practice any of us can ever undertake. In mindfulness, we learn how to be awake and aware, and we learn to accept what is.

Thus we can continuously restore and renew ourselves and refresh our vision of life.

Mindfulness is not something we do every now and then; it is an ongoing practice that deepens with time and spreads out to include every part of our lives. If we sincerely aspire to be wise, we must work at it; if we genuinely aspire to enlightenment, we must make our entire lives into prayers, as St. Paul said. It's not enough to pray every now and then or when we really want something. We can make every breath into a prayer—a mantra and a blessing—if we are conscious of it. Similarly, it is hardly sufficient to meditate for half an hour each day unless you carry that same cultivation of attentive mindfulness into everyday activities, all day long.

Buddhist teachings tell us that if we want to know reality, we need to pay attention to everything we do, in detail, and break it down into the smallest segment of each and every action. We train in being aware of each foot rising and falling as we walk out the door on our way to work. We train in paying attention to our hand movements as we reach for the door and touch and then turn the doorknob, or as we pick up any object, be it a briefcase, purse, pen, scarf, or key. For paying attention truly pays off. It is through incandescent, focused awareness that we can become more wakeful and enlightened.

In this way, we begin to see things just as they are, which is the Buddhist definition of wisdom. Mindfulness is the way we integrate meditation into action. Mindfulness helps us know ourselves better, and thus know the world. Mindful awareness is like wearing a headlamp that illuminates the way whichever direction we look. Through awakened mindfulness, we are never lost or confused. This light never dims.

Mindful awareness gives us the wisdom that will allow us to know the real from the unreal, the darkness from the light, virtue from voice, good from evil, skillful from unskillful, and wholesome from unwholesome. That is why it is sometimes called discriminating wisdom or higher discernment.

Here is a simple six-week program to help us become more mindfully aware and feel more alive and serene. During each of the five weeks, we concentrate on one aspect of mindfulness. This practice is a good way to mingle the Dharma with daily life.

> Week One: Mindfulness of sound
> Week Two: Mindfulness of smell
> Week Three: Mindfulness of sight
> Week Four: Mindfulness of taste
> Week Five: Mindfulness of feeling/sensation
> Week Six: Mindfulness of thought

Although this is a simple practice, it requires patience and attention to detail.

Mindfulness shows us how to make every step with dignity, being fully present and centered while we are going forward. Cultivating this attitude is a significant portion of our training. What we are trying to do is become more wakeful, calm, and clear.

The Buddha taught that we should apply our mindfulness to consciously observe and notice. In this way we begin to understand how we interpret and construct our reality; we begin to understand how we perceive and react to things, people, outer events, and inner feelings; and we start to more clearly see what is going on, thus freeing our minds from delusion and illusion, and eventually giving birth to innate wisdom.

Whether it is through the "ear gate" (hearing") or the "eye gate" (seeing), objects or forms enter, and thus our individual experience occurs. A loud sound, for example, enters our ear gate and we respond. Recognition (or not) occurs, and we label it: "thunder," "door slam," or even "What was that noise?" This is almost immediately followed by subjective, karmically conditioned feelings of liking and disliking—all based upon this almost instantaneous labeling and conceptualizing, as in "nice gurgling brook sounds," or "awful, loud honking car alarm," or even "scary, strange, unfamiliar sound."

Thus our experience is observed to be extremely subjective, a matter of interpretation as much as objective reality. When my mother once visited me in the country, for example, she had a difficult time sleeping because of the unfamiliar silence, which made her nervous. Other city dwellers liked visiting because that deep quietude helped them sleep soundly. Some people love to hear children playing outside their window while others find the exact same sounds distracting and bothersome.

As you begin this practice, whether you are concentrating on sound or taste or smell, try to practice bare attention, which is also known as naked awareness. Be aware of what is entering the sense gate, but don't stray into the next step of labeling or judging. Keep it very precise and simple, one moment at a time.

Choose Your Personal Mindfulness Bell

We start this practice by choosing a particular sound or group of sounds to remind us to experience a moment of mindfulness. In a Buddhist monastery, for example, the sound most often used is that of a mindfulness bell or gong. But since most of us don't live in environments where someone is regularly striking a gong to mark time and activities, we need to improvise.

Here are some sounds that we hear every day that can remind us to practice a moment of mindfulness:

> the meow of a cat
> the barking of a dog
> the honking of a car horn
> the ringing of a phone or doorbell
> the cry of a baby

Choose one or two of these or find another sound that regularly occurs in your environment. Do you hear a subway rumble, for example? Barbara lives near the ocean where she hears gulls crying out to each other. Frank lives near an airport, and large jets fly over his head several times an hour. Try to find a sound that occurs naturally at regular intervals. Don't use more than two sounds because you want to be able to be precise and disciplined; you want to be able to focus on these particular "mindfulness reminders."

Whatever sound you use, this becomes your mindfulness bell. Respond to it as though you are a monk on a silent meditation retreat. Immediately upon hearing the signal sound, drop your thoughts and, if it is at all practical, stop what you are doing. I say "if it is at all practical" because obviously if you are driving a car or piloting a plane, you can't let go of the steering device. The important thing is that you let go of your thoughts, breathe, relax, and center yourself in the present moment. This can certainly be safely accomplished anytime, anywhere, through your conscious intention.

When you hear the sound that you have designated as your mindfulness bell, here is what you do:

> Center yourself in the moment and relax. Let go of
>   your thoughts.
> Just let them come and go and settle down.
> Breathe in through your nostrils.
> Relax and breathe out, saying *Aahhh*.
> Hold out your breath for a moment of emptiness.
> Stay centered, and allow yourself a moment of being,
>   just being
> So simple, so delight-full. So free and easy.

Week One: Mindfulness of Sound

This first week we are concentrating on hearing,
  just hearing.
When you hear your mindfulness bell:

Center yourself in the moment and relax.
Let go of your thoughts.
Just let them come and go and settle down.
Breathe in through your nostrils
Relax and breathe out, saying *Aahhh*.
Hold out your breath for a moment of emptiness.
Stay centered, and allow yourself a moment of being,
 just being
So simple, so delight-full. So free and easy.

As you rest in the moment, are you hearing the sounds around you? Are you suddenly aware of small noises and rustling that you had blocked out? Are you more aware of how your world genuinely sounds?

For a week, do this practice every time you hear your mindfulness bell. This can vastly enhance and transform your awareness of the world.

Week Two: Mindfulness of Smell

In the second week, continue to respond to your mindfulness bell every single time you hear it.

Center yourself in the moment and relax.
Let go of your thoughts.
Just let them come and go and settle down.
Breathe in through your nostrils
Relax and breathe out, saying *Aahhh*.
Hold out your breath for a moment of emptiness.
Stay centered, and allow yourself a moment of being,
 just being
So simple, so delight-full. So free and easy.

Are you aware of the odors entering through the gate of smell? We are all surrounded by a myriad of smells pleasant and unpleasant. Whatever you smell, whether it be your neighbor's homemade soup or the fumes from a passing bus, don't try to define what you smell or describe it. No need to name the smells. Just be and experience them. Let this be the first step to a renewed sense of acceptance.

Week Three: Mindfulness of Taste

Because we are now working on mindfulness of taste, we get to choose a new kind of mindfulness bell. This week, the bell of awareness is going to be a specific taste. To keep it from becoming complicated, choose either sweet or salty to be the bell that reminds you to be mindful of taste. If you were to choose sweet, for example, every time you took your first bite into an apple or took your first sip of a cup of sweetened tea, you would breathe deeply and begin your mindfulness practice.

> Center yourself in the moment and relax.
> Let go of your thoughts.
> Just let them come and go and settle down.
> Breathe in through your nostrils
> Relax and breathe out, saying *Aahhh*.
> Hold out your breath for a moment of emptiness.
> Stay centered, and allow yourself a moment of being,
>   just being
> So simple, so delight-full. So free and easy.

Are you tasting what is in your mouth? Are you aware of both flavor and texture? Just be in the moment, and focus on what is on your tongue. They say that a child's tastebuds are more intensely aware of flavors than those of an adult. As we become more mindful of taste, let's see if we can renew and refresh our awareness of life's flavors and consciously savor them.

Week Four: Mindfulness of Sight

For the fourth week, we are focusing on what we see. Whenever you hear the mindfulness bell, stop what you are doing.

> Center yourself in the moment and relax.
> Let go of your thoughts.
> Just let them come and go and settle down.
> Breathe in through your nostrils
> Relax and breathe out, saying *Aahhh*.
> Hold out your breath for a moment of emptiness.
> Stay centered, and allow yourself a moment of being,
>   just being
> So simple, so delight-full. So free and easy.

Are you seeing? Just notice the forms and colors without labeling or naming anything. Accept what you are looking at without judging. If you are looking at your desk piled high with papers, don't take the next mental step and call it cluttered. If a bird flies by, don't label it bird. Just be aware of the forms, the color, and the movement. Stand in a garden and take in the view of what is. This is what is known as bare awareness. We are learning how to be, just be, as we are. There is no need to add or subtract anything. This is radical acceptance and unconditional openness. This can become transpersonal love.

Week Five: Mindfulness of Feeling

Mindfulness of feeling refers to tactile sensations and bodily awareness. For the fifth week, we are becoming aware of the physical sensations we experience. Whenever you hear the mindfulness bell, stop what you are doing.

> Center yourself in the moment and relax.
> Let go of your thoughts.

> Just let them come and go and settle down.
> Breathe in through your nostrils
> Relax and breathe out, saying *Aahhh*.
> Hold out your breath for a moment of emptiness.
> Stay centered, and allow yourself a moment of being,
>   just being
> So simple, so delight-full. So free and easy.

Are you feeling anything right now? Are you feeling sleepy? Are you feeling hot or cold? Do you feel tight in the chest, stomach, back, neck, feet? Just feel what you feel. Simply feeling what we feel when we're feeling it brings clear perception and valid cognition. It helps us encounter reality. Natural body is Buddhabody—perfect embodiment. Just embody that.

Week Six: Mindfulness of Thought

In the sixth week, we are trying to become more mindful of our thoughts. Mindfulness of thought covers the entirety of consciousness; it covers all our moods and our emotional reactions. We are trying to become aware of what we think and how we think; we are trying to become aware of how we conceptually construct our world and its reality.

Whenever you hear your mindfulness bell, stop what you are doing.

> Center yourself in the moment and relax.
> Let go of your thoughts.
> Just let them come and go and settle down.
> Breathe in through your nostrils
> Relax and breathe out, saying *Aahhh*.
> Hold out your breathe for a moment of emptiness.
> Stay centered, and allow yourself a moment of being,
>   just being
> So simple, so delight-full. So free and easy.

Let the mind settle in its own way, its own place, and its own time. Let thoughts settle, naturally like the ripples on the surface of a placid pond. Natural mind is Buddha's heart-mind, ultimate reality.

This kind of total awareness and unconditional acceptance can refresh our senses and awaken our spirits. This can renew and transform the way we see and experience the world. As we see life afresh, we relinquish old patterns of being; we let go of out-dated behaviors and learn how to dance with life in the present moment. We forget and let go of who we used to be and we are born anew. This is spiritual renewal.

Constant, unwavering application of mindfulness helps us understand that life is full of losses through change and imper-manence. This can help us deal with our sadness; it can also help us experience joy. It can help us renew and transform ourselves and change how we relate to whatever befalls us. This is the spiritual magic of acceptance and equanimity, where we gradu-ally realize that nothing essentially affects our basic existential nature—a truth transcending happiness and sadness, beyond even birth and death.

When we are no longer so tightly identified with who we used to be and how we think things should continue to be—based on the past—every moment of wakefulness is an opportunity to actualize and enjoy our inherent freedom, wholeness, and perfec-tion. The heart-mind is gorgeous in its authentic natural state!

USING THE POWER OF MIND TO TRANSFORM YOUR THOUGHTS

For the last decade or so, the Buddhist magazine, *Tricycle,* has held a day-long event in New York's Central Park called Change Your Mind Day. When Buddhists talk about changing one's mind, we are being very literal. We are talking about altering the way we think. We know that the power of mind can change the way we view everything. We know that we can use the mind to help us deal with our thoughts, no matter how disturbing they may be. We can train our minds and refine our thoughts and attitudes in ways that will positively transform our lives and our world. This is what spiritual practice is actually all about.

After one of my lectures I spoke with a young musician named James. He told me that after his father died, he became so upset that he couldn't even practice his instrument. Upsetting thoughts about his father and his father's illness kept creeping into his head. James's relationship with his father was rocky at best. James always hoped that he and his father would have time to talk and find some resolution for their disagreements, but it never happened. Now, James finds himself having long, drawn-out fantasized discussions and even arguments with his dead father. He imagines what he would say, and he imagines what his father would say. During these conversations, James often becomes angry or sad, and then the feelings linger. James wonders what he can do to help him deal with his distress and free him from the burden of these thoughts and feelings.

Once again, the Buddha actually offered some very practical advice for dealing with disturbing thoughts. These teachings may initially appear simple or even superficial, but they are incredibly helpful. I myself have found it helpful to apply these guidelines and pointers to my own compulsive thinking, excessive worry, or anxiety.

We begin entering into this practice, as always, by relaxing and centering ourselves and breathing in and out gently through our nostrils. In our heads we clearly form the intention that we are going to free our minds of disturbing and obsessive thoughts. We want to feel calm, clear, and at peace with our surroundings and ourselves. We want to find the joyous serenity that is available to us, and we aspire eventually to share that comfort and spiritual solace with other suffering beings.

Read over the following list and reflect on the ways that you can put them into practice in your own life. These five methods were taught by the Buddha himself in a sutra known as *Discourse on the Forms of Thought*.

1. Be Positive

Yes, although the Buddha didn't actually use the words, "use the lemons in your life to make lemonade," that's what he advised. No matter how bad things seem, try to replace your unhappy and negative thoughts with ones that are more joyous, serene, and happy. Look for the bright and sunny kernels of joy in your environment, however small they may seem at the moment, and focus on them. A friend of mine recently told me about her last visit to her grandfather, who was in a nursing home. He was only a few months short of a hundred years old, and he was very frail. He could no longer walk on his own, and his memory wasn't what it used to be. It was winter but the nurses had pushed his wheelchair to sliding glass doors that opened up to the garden in the summer. The nurses told her that he liked to look out at the bluejays and chickadees who gathered at the feeder. "Look at the birds," the elderly man was smiling and beaming. "We have wonderful birds here," he told my friend. "Isn't this a good way to spend an afternoon—looking at the birds."

My friend took her visit to her grandfather as a gentle teaching. There was so little that her grandfather could still do, and yet he focused on the positive and was able to find joy in daily life. Be optimistic about your life and your future, and accept the karma that comes as being beyond your judgment, reaction, or initial impression of it.

2. Be Clear About What Is Hurting You

Reflect on the causes and consequences of what is bothering you. Think about the origins of your difficulty. Did your behavior play a part in your unhappiness? Whenever possible, try to find other ways of behaving that might cause you less grief in the future. Let go of your attachment to old opinions and believing that you are always in the right. Can you accept responsibility and make better choices in the future?

3. Distract Yourself

Let go of any tendency to be obsessive about what is bothering you. Some of my teachers used to advise that we "close our eyes" and avert our gaze from what is bothering us. Think about something else, or do something different to completely change your mind. My teachers also used to say, "Stop feeding the flames of negativity by turning old negative stones over in your head."

4. Question the Way You Think

Pay attention to how you think and what form your thoughts take. Ask yourself what triggered this series of disturbing thoughts. Follow the patterns of thinking that led you to these thoughts. Are you picking and scraping at old scabs and wounds, for example? Think about the different patterns of thought that you could possibly pursue.

5. Push Away the Disturbing Thoughts

If all else fails, use willpower to refocus your mind. Use your inner strength to let go of the particular thought or thoughts that are causing you so much distress. The mind is stronger than we think it is. The power of mind will help you let go of disturbing thoughts, and they will pass on.

TURNING NEGATIVE EMOTIONS
INTO POSITIVE ENERGY

Anger is a very human emotion that we all experience when things are going wrong. I have found that suppressing and repressing anger and dissatisfaction have limited returns, but that doesn't imply that we have to act out our angry impulses. We can find constructive ways to channel these feelings. It's important to remember that conflicting and even negative emotions are only energies, and energy, of course, can be harnessed for positive purposes as well as drive us to harmful actions. One lesson I have learned from working on my own inner anger is how to separate feelings from reactions. If the old saying that anger burns and consumes us is true, I would like to add the corollary that this hot fire can also be used as a rocket-fuel-like propellant for constructive action. We can choose for ourselves how to manage our negative emotions. If we are aware enough, we can turn them into our into allies and put them to work.

There is a wisdom to be found even in anger: With its sharp cutting edge, anger helps us see what may be wrong. Strong emotions can raise our energy and our conscious awareness. We can direct these qualities into positive action. Anger always reminds me that something needs to change or at least be attended to, usually sooner rather than later.

Anger—like any emotion, feeling, or experience—can be a cause for reflection. To the extent that we can tolerate discomfiting feelings instead of suppressing them or insulating ourselves by indulging in habitual behaviors such as eating, drinking, or sleeping, we can pay attention to the feelings long enough to derive some insights from them about what is going on. When we know ourselves better, we are better able to intentionally choose how to respond, instead of being blindly driven as if by a gale wind. I see my own difficult emotions as disruptive children. When they are acting up, it is time to be there for them and with them. I find it best to hang in there and watch the storm blow over. When anger degenerates into hatred and violence, it engenders and perpetuates more of the same.

How can we take anger and turn it into positive energy? My grandmother Anne used to say, "I am so angry I could just scream!" Then she would go and knit furiously until, suddenly, one of her children or grandchildren had a warm sweater or pretty mittens. When I was living in a Tibetan monastery, I found that putting my own upsets into work, such as cleaning, chopping firewood, or building something for the temple, was a good outlet and way to constructively channel inner energy. We have all seen examples of men and women who have turned monumental losses into compassionate movements designed to help their fellow human beings. I'm thinking of organizations like MADD (Mothers Against Drunk Driving) or Alcoholics Anonymous, started by recoveree Bill W.

Energy is like the sleeping giant within us all. Energy is powerful, yet neutral. Whether it helps or hinders us and humanity depends on how we relate to it. Energy can help us open up, or it can make us contract and close down. Vitality, life force, power, creativity, enthusiasm—these are all forms and manifestations of energy. In the beginning was energy. Without energy, nothing can be called into being.

Through mindfulness, as conscious seekers, we can intentionally use the power of mind to help us channel and focus even the most intense and negative feelings into constructive action. Awareness is the way, the truth, and the light.

The fundamental philosophical principle of Buddhism is that all our suffering comes about as a result of an undisciplined mind, and this untamed mind itself comes about because of ignorance and negative emotions. And it is only by applying methods for training the mind that these negative emotions can be dispelled and eliminated. They cannot be removed by some external technique, like a surgical operation.

THE DALAI LAMA,
from *Dzogchen: The Heart Essence of the Great Perfection*

USING THE POWER OF UNCONDITIONAL LOVE TO TRANSFORM YOUR EXPERIENCE

My friend Roberta recently came to the conclusion that she knew very little about love. This insight shocked and surprised her. Roberta, a warm, spontaneous woman, is happily married to a husband she adores. When she first met her husband, her feelings were so intense that they bordered on the obsessional. Roberta feels certain that she loves her parents, her son, her cocker spaniel, and most of her friends. She loves the beach, the color blue, and chocolate ice cream. What would make Roberta feel as though she didn't know all there was to know about love?

Roberta has been reading about Mother Teresa; she also recently finished reading the Dalai Lama's book, *The Art of Happiness*. This has made Roberta realize that, as far as love is concerned, she is still a novice. As much as she loves her family and friends, it isn't totally unconditional. She always expects some kind of payback, no matter how subtle. When she goes out of her way to please her husband, she expects a loving response in return. She loves her parents because they love her. She does favors for her friends because she anticipates some form of quid pro quo. The love she feels for her child is the closest she gets to unconditional love, but even so, she realizes that while she loves her own child, she is pretty lukewarm about children she doesn't know, whether they live around the block or on another continent.

One of the things that kept me studying with Tibetan masters for the last thirty years was an experience of their capacity for unconditional love, which resonated deeply with me and helped me open my own heart. Being loved makes us all more capable of love. In Buddhism when we talk about heart opening and heart awakening, what we are really talking about is love and acceptance. We are talking about learning to open our hearts to everyone.

I like to read the poetry of the Zen saint Ryokan, who lived in Japan two hundred years ago. Ryokan was a Zen master, a poet, a priest, a calligrapher, and a scholar. His home was a small mountainside hut, but he didn't just stay there meditating all day and all night, looking at the moon, like an ordinary hermit. Ryokan loved nature and children. He would come out of his country hut wearing flapping, ragged black robes, looking like an eccentric crow, to play ball with the local children. In the neighborhood, he was known as "the priest who plays with a ball." He always kept a ball in the sleeve or pocket of his capacious robes so if he met any children, he could play with them. In one of his poems, Ryokan wrote: "How happy I am as I go hand in hand with the children." In my favorite poems of his, he said something like, "This old ball in my pocket which I've bounced with children every day is more priceless than the golden Buddha in Daitoko-ji Temple." This is quite a statement of Buddhavision, seeing the Buddha in everything, even playthings.

Obviously it isn't the ball that is more precious than the golden statue of a Buddha, but the love and connection the ball represented. When he looked at the ball, it brought to mind the love he felt for the children and the joy he shared with them. Love was the operative theme in Ryokan's life.

Unconditional love is inseparable from freedom. Pure love is a law unto itself. It is totally proactive, not reactive. Unconditionality frees us from ourselves—from our habitual patterns and hang-ups; it helps set us loose from our fears and limitations. Love creates its own wake, has its own direction, moves according to its own rhythm, and makes its own music. We are all accustomed to thinking in terms of the relational, transactional, give-and-take, business-like experiences, as in you-stroke-me-and-I'll-stroke-you. True love has no sides, limits, or corners. It is without circumference and beyond inside and out. The heart of limitless love includes all and everything, embracing one and all in its warmth. Genuine love is enough in simply being itself.

Love finds its own way and creates its own universe. Loving is the practice of combining selflessness, generosity, and oneness. Loving life in all its forms, even the parts we don't like, frees us from attachment to outdated forms of behavior and beliefs. This keeps us up to date and in the present moment, the fresh immediacy of experience. This holy now, this eternal instant—the moment of total love, freed from fabrication and concept—is the dawn of creation. It births a new world, right amid this one, right here and now. There is no greater freedom or perfection.

LOVE SOMETHING TODAY— A SPIRITUAL PRACTICE

There are so many kinds of love and subtleties of love. I think the word *love*, like *truth* and *God*, is hard to define. And yet who doesn't use this word every day? Here in the West, we tend to associate love mainly with romantic feelings. This is a very limited view. When we talk about "finding love," and pin all our hopes for love on finding a special someone with whom to share romantic feelings, we are limiting our innate capacity for boundless joy and happiness. Without that "special someone" to love who loves us back, we tend to think that we are bereft of love. What a mistake that is! We are all truly surrounded by love. Many can feel that God loves us. Love in all its forms is heartwarming and heart-opening. Divine Buddha-like love does surround and enfold us when we are open to it.

Right now, let's open up our hearts and look beyond romantic love. Let's think about some of the things that we all love even though we may take them for granted. Let's think about how this love can be utilized to fill our hearts, nourish our souls, enrich our experience of life, and renew our spirits. Let's see if we can stretch our capacity for unconditional love. Why not?

We will naturally grow in spiritual wisdom and strength if and when we are able to get out of ourselves and spend a little time every day feeling the joy of love. Try to be spontaneous about this. If you see something you love or are doing something you love, stop for a moment and feel the joy. Experience the non-conceptual, irrational heart-opening. Here are some suggestions about things we could learn to focus on as we learn to love more deeply and unconditionally. Like everything else, we get better at love through practice. Love is as love does.

Love of the Divine

What is faith but another form of love? When we have faith, we have hope for the future. Faith, hope, and love always go together in spiritual teachings; they enhance and support each other. Faith, almost by definition, implies a love of the divine, or of an invisible realm at least. There is no change and transformation possible without some faith. It is this kind of belief in an ultimate order that allows us to take risks; belief allows us to live with hope. Martin Luther King once said, "We must accept finite disappointments, but never lose infinite hope." We are sustained on our journey by an intuitive love of the sacred dimension of life, across all cultural and intellectual borders.

Love of Nature

Look at the cute little birds as they hop about on ledges and branches looking for food; look at the sparkling gulls as they dive into the ocean; look at the humorous ducks as they swim in circles and bob under water and the colorful bluejays and cardinals as they decorate the winter landscape; look at the shy yellow finches and at the chickadees so friendly that they are prepared to take birdseed from your fingers; watch the graceful birds as they swirl and swoop in the sky. Sometimes when I'm in the countryside I see what appears to be hundreds of swallows flying together making loop the loops and figure-eights in the sky. What a sight! Who made all this? one wonders.

Nature is all around us, even in the big city. Close your eyes and listen to the sound of rain. Close your eyes and feel the breezes. Put your face up to the heavens and look at the stars or feel the soft snow as it lands on your cheeks. Walk in the park in spring and smell a lilac bush. Don't you love that smell? Buy a plant, put it in a sunny window, and love and nurture it. Love nature and use that love to renew your senses and your awareness of the joys of life.

Love Children

Even if you don't have any children or grandchildren of your own, there are other children in the world who need to be loved and embraced. Volunteer at a hospital; volunteer with the Big Brothers or Big Sisters. Just about every community has some way that you can develop a positive, wholesome relationship with boys and girls. When I take a young child to a movie or a zoo or the park, I feel like a kid again myself; it changes my experience and it changes my view. I have a neighbor who is six years old. He and I share a birthday even though we are separated by several decades. I travel about the country quite a bit, and one of the things I look forward to when I'm coming home is hanging out with my six-year-old friend. This year he likes to wear armor and duel; last year he got three rabbits; dinosaurs used to be huge in his life. Who knows what's next? These are renewing experiences.

Love Animals

People fall in love with animals. There are so many needy animals in the world. In your own locale, no matter where it is, there are probably organizations and groups who are caring for homeless animals that need help. If you don't want to take one home, you can probably still volunteer to walk a dog or help take care of a cat. Dogs give us so much devotion and loyalty in return for our care. My wife, Kathy, has an Abyssinian cat who allows us to share his space and admire his beautiful fur. We just got a honey-colored puppy named Lili.

Love Creativity, Beauty, and Art

Open up to art, music, dance, or poetry. Let your heart and soul soar to the sounds of Beethoven, Mozart, or even Willie Nelson. We all love some form of music, don't we? Indulge that love. There are valid reasons why music is often such an important part of the sacred experience.

Music transports me. Doesn't it make your spirit shine? Love art; love music; love dance; love poetry. What we really love is the splendor of the creative imagination.

Love Knowledge

Love books and all forms of learning. Learning something new can't help but expand our horizons and give us a fresh outlook on life. Learning keeps us young and helps us grow and transform. Not only does learning provide inspiration, it often produces practical results. Margaret went back to school at fifty-six, graduated at sixty, and in her early sixties has a brand-new career as a hospital planner. Susan, who had been a successful accountant, went back to school when she was sixty and got a Master of Social Work degree. Now she is a practicing social worker, working with people instead of numbers and computers. Don't be afraid to commit yourself to learning more about a subject you love. Learning helps us stretch and refresh our brain cells and renew our mental credit cards so we don't come up empty. Keep learning.

Love Your Personal Interests and Hobbies

Appreciate and honor the things that make you unique. Keep doing them. My friend Nancy is, by her own description, a less than talented pianist. Yet she continues to practice every day because she loves it. It gives her pleasure and helps her relax and cope with life's difficulties. What a loss it would have been for her if she stopped playing simply because she had relatively little innate talent! Bob loves softball; he's sixty-eight-years old and plays in a senior league. He felt a little foolish about responding to the newspaper announcement that a senior league was forming, but now he is so delighted that he got past that knee-jerk response. Baseball and his new teammates have greatly enhanced his life. Whatever it is that you have always wanted to do—from painting with watercolors to fly fishing—do it and love it! You will feel renewed.

Love Humanity

Think about Mother Teresa and how much love she gave and also received in her life. Love your neighbors; love your coworkers; love your family; love strangers; love those who need your compassion and help. And yes, of course, love your adversaries and enemies too, because they have lessons in store for you and are among your greatest teachers.

Love Work

What a joy and blessing it is to be able to love and enjoy work. Don't hold back on your focus, skill, talent, and enthusiasm. Do what you do with love and commitment. If you can't openheartedly love what you do every day for money, try to find work or a craft that you can wholeheartedly pursue as a pleasurable hobby.

⁓

When you realistically list and think about everything and everybody that can be loved, it's obvious that the whole world is filled with love. The entire spectrum of love can be experienced by any of us here and now, in this very world, within our lifetimes. We have a lot of love to give and the more we can love, the more we receive. So embrace the concept of love, open your heart, and be transformed. You'll love it.

THE TRANSFORMATIVE ENERGY OF UNCONDITIONAL LOVE AND ACCEPTANCE

One of Tibet's most beloved lamas of the past was Patrul Rinpoche, who lived from 1808–1887. He was a poor and scraggly vagabond. Nonetheless, Tibetans revere him as an enlightened master because he left behind a legacy of warm and practical wisdom. For most of his life, Patrul Rinpoche wandered in the Himalayas, living in the wilderness, sleeping in isolated caves, where he spent his time meditating and teaching. He had few possessions other than the clothes on his back, his teapot, and a walking stick. In his head he carried the words of Shantideva's classic, known in the West as *The Way of the Bodhisattva,* which he had memorized in its entirety. Patrul Rinpoche taught the entire book at least one hundred times. Legend has it that once he even taught it to an unseen array of ghosts at a haunted villa at the request of local villagers.

The Dalai Lama often refers to Patrul Rinpoche's teachings, and uses almost the same words as he did to transmit the essential message: Nothing is more important than cultivating a good heart; nothing is more important than acting with kindness to others. My teachers always told stories about Patrul Rinpoche's life. They said that throughout his days, when he prayed, his prayers for others were as fervent as those he spoke for himself. I was taught that this prayer from Shantideva was one of Patrul's favorites.

> In all my future lives
> May I never fall under the influence of evil companions;
> May I never harm even a single hair of any living being;
> May I never be deprived of the sublime light of Dharma.

May whoever has been connected to me in any
   possible way
Be purified of even the most serious sins;
May he or she close the doors to lower rebirth,
And be born in Chenrayzig's blissful Buddhafield,
   Dewachen.

Patrul Rinpoche's life exemplified generosity; whenever he was given money or offerings, he quickly handed them over to others, giving generously to the poor and the homeless. It is said that there was little that Patrul Rinpoche loved more than being able to give to others. A favorite story my teachers told concerns a man who approached the learned teacher and begged him for some money.

"Oh my poor friend," Patrul said. "Just say to me, I don't need any money, and I will give you some."

The beggar thought that he had been misunderstood, so he repeated his request for money. Once again Patrul answered, "Just say to me, I don't need any money, and I will give you some."

Finally the man uttered the sentence Patrul had been requesting. "I don't need any money," he said. Patrul in turn rewarded him with a handful of silver coins.

Then Patrul told the beggar the following story about Lord Buddha.

It seems that one day as the Buddha traveled through India, a poor man came up to him and gave the Buddha the only gift he had, a single piece of milk sugar candy. As the Buddha was looking at the candy and wondering what to do with it, another man, known for his greedy inclinations, saw the candy in Buddha's hand and asked if he could have it. The man, of course, knew that the generous Buddha never said "no" to such a request.

The man was quite surprised when the Buddha did not immediately hand over the candy. Instead the Buddha spoke to the man, saying:

"Just say to me, I don't need this milk sweet. And then I shall give it to you."

The man did as the Buddha requested, and he got the candy, which he promptly popped into his mouth.

Later the Buddha's disciples asked the Buddha why he wanted the man to say those words.

"Because," the Buddha replied, "through hundreds of lifetimes this man has never even once said the words, *I don't need.* By saying these few simple words, he may have momentarily experienced the feeling of needing nothing. These words undermine greed, and may help plant the seeds of generosity."

Padma Sambhava, the great Indian master who introduced Buddhism to Tibet in the eighth century, told his disciples that when asked, they should say, "I don't know, I don't want, I don't need." I try to remember that.

This is a lesson in nonattachment and acceptance. It is a lesson in learning to love unconditionally without expecting results, rewards, or payment of any kind. It may feel counterintuitive, but acceptance does have a transformative effect. Nonattachment and acceptance have their own magic and can transform anything. Letting go is the ultimate act of generosity and faith. And every good deed is a gift to both giver and recipient.

> *Be kind to the destitute,*
> *Be patient and loving toward the wicked,*
> *Be kind to the afflicted,*
> *Be gentle with the fool,*
> *Empathize with the weak and oppressed,*
> *Be especially compassionate to those who cling to concrete reality.*

PATRUL RINPOCHE

Spiritual renewal is all about energy, attitude, and outlook. How to renew yourself? Join me early each morning in going outside to greet the day and see what has been created anew. And meet the dogs and their people, and all the other seekers out on their morning pilgrimages. Meet each day like a renewed life.

Acknowledgments

I wish to gratefully acknowledge Christopher Coriat and Leah Weiss for computer help, Ron Goldman for tape recording, and Roz Stark for transcribing; Hal Ross, Paul Crafts, and John Makransky for suggestions; Julie Barker, Kate Miller, Betty Holmes, Corey Flanders, Camille Hykes, and Vince and Lucy Duggan for research. To Trace Murphy at Doubleday Broadway, my perfect editor, and my dear literary agent, Susan Cohen; and to Julia Coopersmith, who provided patient assistance on this book, thank you. And to my wife, Kathy Peterson, for invaluable support and encouragement.

Index

About the

DZOGCHEN CENTER

More information about Lama Surya Das and his schedule of lectures, workshops, retreats, tapes, CDs, local meditation groups, and Dzogchen training can be found at:

www.surya.org

Those without Internet access, please write or call:

The Dzogchen Center
P.O. Box 400734
Cambridge, MA 02140
(617) 628-1702

To order a CD of companion chants called *Chants to Awaken the Buddhist Heart*, by Lama Surya Das and Steven Halpern, contact the Dzogchen Center at the above address or at www.dzogchen.org.

DZOGCHEN
FOUNDATION

About the Author

An authorized lama in the Dzogchen lineage of Tibet, Surya Das is a sought-after spiritual teacher and meditation master, poet, and spokesperson for the emerging American Buddhism. Founder of the Dzogchen Center, he is also the author of several popular books, including *Awakening the Buddha Within, Awakening to the Sacred,* and *Awakening the Buddhist Heart,* which comprise his bestselling Awakening Trilogy, the first trilogy of Buddhism for the West. He also writes regularly for *Tricycle* magazine and Beliefnet.com, is active in interfaith dialogue, and is a founder and board member of several Buddhist monasteries, centers, and charitable projects in refugee camps in Asia and the West. He lives outside Boston, Massachusetts.